An insight into the Pros and Cons
of Home-Schooling

HATED SCHOOL
LOVED HOME-SCHOOLING

A guide for parents of autistic children

ALANA MONET-TELFER

ACKNOWLEDGEMENTS

This beautiful piece of autobiography literature would not have even come to fruition without first my lovely mum being there.

My mum has helped me through a lot emotionally, physically and psychologically. Without my mum's guidance and close watch, there would be no author to write this story and share to the world. I would also like to thank my sister who was the main person of encouragement and pushed me to keep going. Siblings are amazing people, and I am glad I have one; my sister!

Thank you, Mum!

I am so happy and grateful that I received the help from Sutton College, and their two members Jo Fenwick and Gill Heath. It has been a pleasure working with them from the start to the finish of the manuscript, including gaining valuable advice, and heart felt compliments. Thank you so much Jo and Gill for being there for me and helping me along with my mother.

By receiving love, care, and guidance from these people, I have learned what a true author should be, and what a true person devoted on their life purpose should be like; therefore, embodying those people myself, and becoming an author/ spiritual being completing one of their many life purposes.

I would like to thank Vicky and Staff from Follow Your Dreams. Follow Your Dreams is a national charity operating in England and Wales that inspires children and young people with learning disabilities to follow their dreams.

Their vision is for children and young people with learning disabilities to recognise their potential, be ambitious and be provided with the opportunities to follow their dreams. The charity focuses on children's abilities, growing and developing skills through the delivery of creative and interactive events, community groups and workshops.

Finally, I would like to thank Chris who has given use the time and has practiced the most beautiful attitude of patience, to get this book published. From the core of my heart, I thank everyone.

I love you all.

Published by
Filament Publishing Ltd
16, Croydon Road, Beddington, Croydon,
Surrey, CR0 4PA, United Kingdom
www.filamentpublishing.com
+44(0)20 8688 2598

© 2018 Alana Monet-Telfer
ISBN 978-1-912256-50-1

The right of Alana Monet-Telfer to be recognised as the author of this work has been asserted by her in accordance with the Designs and Copyrights Act 1988.

All rights reserved.
No portion of this work may be copied without the prior written permission of the publisher.

Printed by IngramSpark.

Table of Contents

About the Author	6
Introduction	7
Chapter 1: My Story	9
Chapter 2: Influences	29
Chapter 3: Bullying	40
Chapter 4: My Bully	69
Chapter 5: Home-schooling Begins	94
Chapter 6: Prejudices and Myths	109
Chapter 7: Challenges of Home-school	121
Chapter 8: My Exam Years	151
Chapter 9: Ready for Home-school?	167
Chapter 10: The Purpose of this Book	179
Reference/Web links	186
Appendix	191

About the Author
Alana Monet-Telfer

Student, Author and Entrepreneur

I don't fit into other people's worlds. I create my own world.

Alana Monet-Telfer is a British born self-published author and writer who has been writing books for over five years. Over the past decade, Alana has been an entrepreneur, selling her art work and having her own two YouTube channels where she publishes her life and content. In her life as a writer, Alana has published educational books from applied science to business, skincare and cooking books. Her most famous book is "The Benefits of Nature" which can be found on Amazon.

Alana has always been independent, strong willed and an achiever in her life. This has reflected in her grades, which have been straight distinctions, as well as in her hobbies. Examples of these are her passion for spoken word poetry and the thirst for knowledge in the topics of property investment, business and spirituality.

Alana's motto in life is always to create her reality and, no matter how much hardship hits her, never to give up and to persevere on to her next milestone of success.

Introduction

This is not any old book. This book is one of my most prized possessions, which took blood, sweat, tears, pain and four years to complete. You may wonder why this book took so much of me to create; let alone why I would go through so much to create something which almost destroyed me. The reason is because it was all about me and the demons I faced.

This book contains the story of my childhood as a home-schooled child with Autism and Expressive and Receptive Language Disorder. I realized my childhood was a massive struggle and I faced many challenges that an average child might not have faced. Feeling   I can help someone else with my story and experiences, as well as being now at the age of twenty,

I have decided to create an insight/autobiographical book to help children, home-schooled children, parents who know nothing about home-schooling, parents who may be thinking of home-schooling and parents who are already home-schooling learn from my life experiences and hopefully be able to help them make the most important decisions of their lives.

ANALYSIS THOUGHT

At the end of all the chapters of this book, I'll have Analysis Thoughts, which analyse the chapter, lessons from my experiences, the events of my experiences and tips on what to do to face some of the challenges which I experienced. I know some of the experiences and problems explained here in this book don't happen just to a home-schooled child, but can happen to anyone of any age.

Therefore, I hope these solutions can one day help you, if you ever fall into the same, or similar, situations I have had in my life. This is not a bible for what to do when you want to home-school your children. Therefore, it is best to take heed of this book, as well as to research the subject in full detail before making your own decision.

Chapter 1: My Story

My story all began in Mayday Hospital. A baby girl, who was four days late, was born weighing eight pounds. This baby was me; I am the youngest of my family and have two other siblings. Out of my parents, my mother was the one who had helped me the most, and nurtured me from a helpless new-born, into a fully-fledged, confident and organized seventeen-year-old teenager. I was born with two disabilities and those were Receptive and Expressive Language Disorder followed by Autism.

Receptive and Expressive Disorder

This is when the child, such as me, has difficulties expressing him or herself using spoken or written language. Even to this day, although my vocabulary has increased immensely, I still have some difficulty trying to explain what I mean to someone, using spoken or written words. Therefore, this also happens when it comes to answering certain questions, such as comprehension questions. When I get muddled with words or meanings, I always refer to a thesaurus, or ask my mother what a word means. The symptoms of this disorder can be that the child cannot follow instructions as clearly or as precisely as they want to or are told to, have trouble recalling words, constructing coherent sentences and using and constructing grammar. All these symptoms occur because the child's understanding is misinterpreted or misunderstood.

Another symptom of this disorder is that the child could have trouble socializing with others and making friends, not because the child does not want to, but because it is difficult for them to know how to communicate and make friendships. Here is an example...

Let's set the scene. You are at a birthday party and you see a lot of kids running around, chatting and laughing and you want to join in too. However, with Receptive and Expressive Language Disorder, your social interaction with people is delayed. You go over to the kids and say, "Hi" or something as simple as that. However, when trying to play with them or get into their conversation, your expressive self is restrained, you feel closed and confused, because you are not sure how to get into their conversation or games. Therefore, it can be very upsetting and distressing for a child with that type of disorder.

With Receptive Disorder, it is how the child hears or understands words that can affect them. They could have trouble pronouncing certain words, or are not sure how to respond appropriately to a certain situation or statement. Receptive Disorder can also make a child's idea of a connection of word different from its true meaning. Here is another example...

I was at a special carer's party, and my mother was encouraging me to socialize, as she always did whether I stayed with her for a long time or kept to myself in another room. I was ten years old at the time. Finally, after combating my psychological fear to go up to people, I had the courage to go up to a group of girls and talk to them. They seemed to be giggling at me and I was not sure why but, to please my mother, I continued to try to make conversation, ignoring the small fits of laughter coming from some other girls in the group. Finally, one of them stated quietly that, "Your flies are down." Now of course this means that your trouser zipper is down, and, unfortunately, your undergarment can be seen. However, I had never heard this way of speech before, and instead of looking down at my trousers, I repeated it again as I was confused because I didn't know exactly what she meant. I thought she meant that real flies were down, and I didn't register its true meaning, until my mother came over and told me that my trouser zipper was low and needed to be zipped up.

It sounds very foolish now, but this is an example of how words can be misunderstood by some

Receptive Disordered children. For the rest of the party I was deeply embarrassed and stayed by myself for the rest of the afternoon. It was the first time I socialized properly, or at least tried to. For me, that misunderstanding was a great failure but, in life, we must continue even if we fail.

Autism

Autism is a very well-known disorder; however, it is not fully talked about. It seems to me that, only last year, the subject of Autism has suddenly been spoken about and analysed.

My Understanding of Autism

Autism is a spectrum disorder. It also means a unique and peculiar reconstruction of the neural development growth. Therefore, Autism affects the brain information processing of a child, by alternating how the nerve cells and their synapses connect and organize certain data. What occurs in the child's mind is not fully understood by others when the child, or person, with Autism is trying to express or explain something to them. This can be explained in more simple terms as a lifelong developmental disability. Autism can have effects on a child, some good and some bad. On the unfortunate side, Autism can make some people impaired in normal actions or functions, as well as become impaired in social interaction and communication. Some signs of Autism have been found in a child when they are….

Giving no eye contact:

I do not mean the normal ignoring eye contact. No eye contact in a child with Autism is when the child will not look at you while you are speaking to them or trying to make conversation and this is repeated. At the age of five, I had a challenging time looking at my teachers, adults and parents in the eye; therefore, they thought I was purposely ignoring them, which got me into quite a bit of trouble.

Unaware of their surroundings or people:

This symptom is when a child is deeply infatuated in another object or sight, so much that when you call them or are trying to make a conversation, they either will not give eye contact, show no signs of knowing you are there or won't respond at all. It is as if they have drifted into space or are deeply daydreaming. Children can do this normally but, if the same thing is constantly happening, no matter whether it's you trying to gather their attention or somebody else is trying to, don't just ignore it. They can be unaware of their surroundings and people if they are deeply engaged or engrossed in a certain sight or object. It can be very bright colours, toys, animals or even their own hands. It can be anything which makes them unaware of their surroundings and people trying to socialize with them. Therefore, this unfortunately increases their impaired communication and socialization.

Unaffectionate/don't want any affection:

Children, especially those of younger age, love to be hugged or cuddled by their parents. However, another sign of Autism can be when they are the complete opposite. No matter what, they do not want to be hugged, touched or have any physical interaction with anyone, not even their parents. Even to this day, I still have a terrible time when it comes to being touched. It makes me feel uncomfortable, feel vandalised and my skin feels like it's crawling all over my body.

Having no friends for an unusual period: if the child does not have any friends, for example, from the age of 5 till 16 or so on, it may be a sign that the child may have a spectrum of Autism.

Doesn't know how to express or talk about his/her feelings:

At the worst of times we need someone to turn to in order to let out our sorrows, but it's even worse when you don't know how to express them to another person in a way they will understand. This symptom connects with the Expressive Disorder mentioned earlier, where a child can have trouble expressing him or herself, in this case, spoken language. I had the most painful time trying to say how I felt, only for my mother to tell me to try again and think slowly before explaining my thoughts. She meant this in the kindest way possible, but when you're a child that knows you have a small communication problem, and feels like an outcast from the world, it doesn't seem to be understood in a caring light and it made me stressed even more.

These are just the few symptoms of an Autistic child, and to explain every single symptom of Autism would take a long time for you to read. The best thing is to research Autism and find out more about it. Take the symptoms to heart too, just in case you have a child, nephew, grandson, granddaughter or niece who shows some of these symptoms, or if you already have a child showing one or more signs of these abnormal social behaviours. Not only will your child be thankful for you finding out if they have any disabilities, but also it will save them the pain and suffering of feeling like a displaced person in the future.

Mild Autism

Mild Autism is the same as Autism, except the disorder is not as strong. Some of the symptoms can show, but not be as extreme as a low functioning autistic child. This is what I have: I have High Functioning Autism, which is where the signs and effects are not visible, unless you get to know me or are around me for long enough to see. It is also known as the invisible disability. Going back to the topic of Mild Autism, to help you understand Mild Autism a little more, I'll explain the mild autistic symptoms. These are...

Not understanding common phrases and their meanings;

There are some meanings of phrases I don't understand even to this day like "A rolling stone gathers no moss" or a more well-known one just like "As you sow so shall you reap". Those are just the few examples of not understanding a certain phrase and its meaning. After hearing those I researched them; so, when they were repeated next time in future; I won't feel unsure about how to react to what is being said.

Being unaware of my surroundings;

I had this symptom at a younger age at around three years old. Remember when I stated that a certain sight or object can distract a child from their surroundings? For me it was a toy piggy which I carried with me everywhere. I loved the piggy very much and played with it all the time. My mother told me when

I grew out of the farm animal toys, that when I was engrossed with my piggy, nothing else seemed to attract me, not my mother's voice calling me, nor any other toy.

Misinterpretation of non-verbal language:

Body language is one form of non-verbal language which may not be understood in certain Autistic Spectrum or Mildly Autistic children. The rolling of eyes which means sarcasm was a non-verbal language which I didn't truly recognize, as well as my mother's look at me if I said something wrong or something that was not meant to be said. Fortunately, I've grown to realize mum's silent warnings and other people's non- verbal language, because my mother and elder sister warned me about it and about how kids can use it either for good or for bad. For example, some people can use non-verbal language to take advantage of someone or be cruel to them.

Having a literal understanding of language:

The most problems I had at social events and home-school were separating which comments were meant as a joke and which were meant in a serious light. For example...

The word "Silly" is normally said to a person who is not on the ball in a certain situation, or has made a small mistake, which can be easily brushed off and sorted. For me, the word 'silly' in my school was used more harshly as in the term of "Don't be so stupid." After my mother took me out of the school, she was teaching me maths one day, when I made a small mistake on one of my sums and my mother replied jokingly, "Whoops, that was a silly answer, let's try again..." The words struck though me like sharpened daggers and my heart swelled up as if fit to burst. I thought she meant I was a stupid person, that my thinking was completely dumb and inexperienced. My mother looked at me in surprise and wondered why I had suddenly changed. After crying and telling her, she told me that she didn't literally think I was stupid, it was just a joke.

I can't stress enough to parents out there with children, or autistic children, to please be careful with your words when using certain phrases with them. Words can be cutting to the soul and to the growth of a child. If you call them stupid or another type of degrading word, without any light emphasis or explanation, it can psychologically affect the child, hinder their spirit and make them feel less worthy then they felt before. For an autistic child, the effect hits them ten times harder mentally (because we are very sensitive and emotional more than the neurotypical people) than it does for a child without Autism. Other words which an autistic child can take as literal meanings could be...

- "Pay though the nose"

- "Walking on eggshells"

- "Take a rain check"

As I stated above, there are not only negative things about Autism, but also very beneficial and positive things too.

Atypical Autism/ Pervasive Development Disorder

This was the type of Autism which I was specifically diagnosed with. Atypical Autism is a spectrum of Autism that can be undiagnosed for years; however, luckily this did not happen to me, since it would have caused a lot more stress and problems in the future. People with Atypical Autism might experience or have certain spectrums of the three types of Autism; however, it will not fit the overall condition of Autism itself. For a child with Atypical Autism; these are the types of symptoms they can have:

- No to little eye contact.
- Vocabulary building and understanding vocabulary.
- Not understanding nonverbal language (crossed arms means defensive, but some people with Autism may not understand about personal space.)
- A strong difficulty to learning how to make friends, as well as naturally not knowing the social mechanism of how to make friends.
- Limited speech to being mute.

- Strong sensitivity to sounds, noises, lights, touch, or any other of the five senses. This results in meltdowns, anxiety attacks, and depression.
- Repeating a certain routine over and over, which can result in OCD.
- Having a lot of emotion, but not being able to physically show or communicate it to others. This can make them people with Autism look emotionless; when they are not.

Pervasive Development Disorder

This is where the child has very mild symptoms of Autism; however, this does not mean that they have actual Autism, or are autistic. People with Pervasive Development Disorder also do have problems socializing and communication skills; hence, this includes verbal and non-verbal communication.

Positives of Autism

Even though Autism affected me with social, body language and recognition problems, I still benefitted in other ways and I really want to bring out the positives of Autism to children and adults alike so they won't mistake it for just an unfortunate case or unlucky disorder. Some of the benefits of Autism in a child can be…

- **Increased Memory:**

The child can have a much better increased memory, than the average person. This does not only happen in Autism but in other disorders such as ADHD. This is one of my benefits with mild Autism and it helps me when remembering steel pan notes in music class plus the timing. I can play "What a Wonderful World" without any music paper beside me. The notes and timing flow into my head like a favourite song.

A small tip is that, if you forget something, whether it be a method on a maths paper or a chord on a piano; repeat, ask for help, and once you find the solution or the right chord, keep repeating it until it melts into your memory like butter on a frying pan. Increased memory has helped me with Maths, English and even simple things, for example, remembering a message that needs to be given to my mum later if she's not in the house.

- **Control over their Emotions:**

Not all Autistic people or children will have a deeper control over their feelings. It's natural that sometimes our emotions can override us, especially bad ones, but I know this is one of the benefits I have that has helped me to understand the world and have a calmer understanding of others. At school my bully name was Banana. It hurt for a while, I admit that; however, after being entered in the second year of school, the name didn't rock my emotional boat at all. Back then I thought it was a ridiculous name, and there was really no point crying over that. Now I realised that the bullies in that school only did the name-calling and other symptoms of bullying so they could be cool in front of their so-called peers, who were bullies themselves. Therefore, it has made me not feel upset by it. If I get called any rude names or given labels, I just ignore them and move on.

- **Unique Insight and Imagination:**

It has been stated that children with Autism have a different view of life, whether it's of what is important to them to a film; Autistic children have a different insight and view of something. When I was younger, I loved creating little play sets and toys for myself using pure junk like paper, toilet rolls, pens for colouring and almost anything else. For example…

In my youth, my imagination sparked with many ideas and creations. One day I found a bottle, paper, string and a toy cap that looked like the bottom of an acorn cup but a bit larger (Kinder Egg toy caps). What possible invention could I create with this? Seems like nothing right now, but with some work, a few trials and errors and spillage of water from the tap, I could create a little toy well. I even made a hole in the cup so the water would flow in but, really, I should have used a small stone to make it heavy enough. This is one example of creative insight and imagination. I thrived more in my Art GCSE afterwards and got a very good grade.

- **Focus:**

The power to focus on a goal or mission and never give in until it's finished. I remember working for my IGCSE's and focusing on my work every day. I was a perfectionist, my homework had to be done at a certain time otherwise I would feel guilty for the rest of the day; I even worked at 1am in the morning because my passion to get it done and learn burned brightly.

- **Maturity:**

For me I achieved maturity, hence, at the age of 16 I was complimented, saying I had the mindset of an eighteen to nineteen-year-old young adult. This was all due to observing the way my mum talked with people, and then adapting it to my own environment. My mum did have to help me to decide which environment I used my mature mindset in, since when I met new home-school kids, I would shake their hand with a firm grip instead of just saying "Hi." If your child, whether they have Autism or not, has a mature mindset and personality, don't hinder that gift or try to get rid of it. If anything, encourage them to use it but also tell them which environments it would be most appropriate to use it in.

Analysis Thought: Chapter 1

This chapter goes into the background information of how everything started. How could a story begin without the protagonist? I would like you, the reader, to get to know me before continuing the story of my life, as well as the disability I have. The main point of this chapter was to go into Autism/Mild Autism and decipher it, so it can be clearer to people who never heard of it before or don't understand it clearly.

In my first analysis, I would like to offer some friendly advice about disabilities and what could and in some cases should be done if one is discovered. The first and most important one is...

- **Don't ignore it:**

Finding that your child has a disability is hard for any parent to cope with. It might be hard to adjust and learn to live with; however, what I can't stress enough is PLEASE DON'T IGNORE IT! Don't act as if it's not present, that your child could have a disability and is showing symptoms and yet you brush it off or think it's a temporary phrase. Disabilities like this, can have the most devastating impact on a child's life in the future. You would be the one to regret it if the child is either disconnected from life, has psychological, mental and emotional problems or comes back to tell you what you should have done and that you failed them by not being loving, understanding, accepting and supportive. I've seen this in many places; people ignoring the symptoms of their child who shows symptoms of a possible kind of disability. One child whose parents were ignoring him showed the symptoms. With him it was unawareness of surroundings; whether he was playing or just walking around, and the constant engrossed attention with his fingers. Apart from these symptoms, he was a very loving boy.

- **Feel Proud:**

OK so you find out that your child, or maybe you yourself, have Autism, ADHS, AS or Sickle Cell, but it doesn't mean it's the end of the world. It does not mean that you're nothing, and should crawl into the deepest dark end of a cave. Don't ever let anyone make you think that. You and other children born on this earth were born for a reason, and yes maybe it's unknown right now, but everyone is unique whether they have a disorder or not and it should be acknowledged. Unfortunately, in this world it is not, and sometimes people are ridiculed for it or are treated differently. What I can tell you is that there are famous people who have Autism and I'll show a few.

Lewis Carroll: The author of Alice in Wonderland and the sequel book: Through the Looking Glass.
Charles Darwin: He is associated with the theory of evolution.

Albert Einstein: Scientist and physicist

Jane Austen: The writer of the books Pride and Prejudice and Sense and Sensibility.

- **Love your child/ Love yourself:**

Knowing that you have confidence will stop others dead in their tracks when they try to break you. Self- esteem and confidence are the most powerful tools needed to face this world when dealing with people. Without them, we would be lost and let ourselves be beaten by other people who probably don't even have confidence in themselves either. Learn to love yourself, find a diary, and write at least one thing that you like about yourself every day and, as you do, your confidence will grow.

If you are a parent with a child who has a disability, let them know how great they are. Tell them that they are good and compliment them on at least one thing. Don't just say a random compliment every day, but when they do something good, or feel like they're worthless, just tell them how great they are, how they are brilliant in their hobbies or work.

Give them the strength to know that they are special and that's all that matters to you, so they can continue dealing with the world.

Chapter 2: Influences

Before I was home-schooled, I was in the Expressive and Receptive Language Disorder centre of a school, which for me was the only good place I enjoyed learning and school experience.

The reason why I dedicate this book to my mother is because my mother fought through almost everything for my well-being. Before I even got a place in the centre, my mother had to fight to get me the spot. She not only faced the false lies from the teachers after I was sent into the mainstream school system, but also, the rejection from my father's side of the family including my father himself.

It all began when my mother was trying to find a space for me in the Expressive and Receptive Language centre. This was when my mother's hard- core determination came in and she fought solidly for my place in the language centre. I really do thank my mother for always fighting for me. She had the trickiest and most stressful time with my father, whose pride had consumed him so much that any mention of a disability of any sort in connection in his family would have been shameful and would be treated as unacceptable. He always said that I didn't have anything, that my mother was being too over the top and she should have just put me into the mainstream system.

Fortunately, my mother knew better. Finally, my mother won the battle. It seemed I was a liability to the school. I knew that to grow just like a seed, I still needed to start from there and I'm glad I had a loving strong parent who did it for me.

Neglect

Neglect: A passive form of abuse in which the perpetrator is responsible to provide care for a victim who is unable to care for oneself, but fails to provide adequate care to meet the victim's needs, thereby resulting in the victim's demise.

Neglect can happen anywhere. It can happen in the neglect of a dog because the person won't care or does not want to care for them or the neglect of a partner because the other half is not attracted to them anymore. As for me: the term of 'neglect' is when a child with a disability is almost disowned because, to the other person, knowing them would cause stress or that they just can't accept them for who they are.

Neglect from my Father's side

In the beginning of Chapter One, I went over how ignoring a child with a disability, as well as acting like they don't have any at all, can be the most damaging action to do to a child. Unfortunately, this is what my father did. His neglect of my disability (and trying to cover it up) caused my mum to feel even more alone in the battle for me. Now that I'm sixteen and know that my father tried to cover it all up, I don't see him in a good light any more, nor do I appreciate him as my father at all. Unfortunately, in 1996 my parents divorced. When my mother gave birth to us and asked if he could fulfil his responsibility for taking care of us while she worked, he didn't want to let go of his apparent single life. That caused the first crack in their marriage and affected their relationship in the long run. It was mostly due to the neglect of responsibility for me and my sister's care from my father that caused the break up. Painfully I must add there was also infidelity and after my mother found out she wouldn't take it anymore, therefore, they got divorced. When I was younger I thought it was my fault that it happened, that my disability caused them to split. I used to cry to myself, feeling sick inside and lonely. My mother was there to comfort me, to show me it was not my fault at all, and that it was a choice made by them and not because of my disability at all. Since then my father comes to visit me and my sister on Sundays.

Although he still comes to see me and my elder sister; the bond between me and my father has totally vanished. To know that my own father was trying to cover up the fact of my disabilities, which were sorted and helped by my home-school community, and still felt comfortable sending me into a school system which would otherwise have ruined me if I didn't get any help, just to save face, was a real stab in the back. When my mother finally got me that place in the language centre, my father's side of the family became sour and turned against my mother in the cruelest sinister ways possible. The most poisonous manipulator and trouble-maker of my father's side was my grandmother, who is meant to be sweet and understanding. However, to this day she's the complete opposite, a depressed lonely woman who has nothing better to do than to make others miserable, chat behind her own daughter's back, and has a possessive mental control over my father.

Control and Manipulation from my Grandmother. My grandmother's mental control over my father was really sickening to experience, and still is to this day. My father somehow can't live at least one week without seeing her, unless his work is overtaking him and becomes too important for him to come down to see her. Other than that, if he was ok with his time and work, we had to visit her every single Sunday which at first was ok. However, when you keep doing this over and over for sixteen years, and having to hear a lady who can only talk about ghosts haunting her and her home, plus her dangerously emotional comments about death, another visit to her home is unbearable. My grandma made me mentally depressed. Even her pet bird even died early because it could not take her presence any more. It has even made me want to stop seeing my father altogether because of it. There was one event explained by my mother, to which I never, even to this day, can forgive my father and grandmother for.

My mother needed to go into hospital to have her tonsils removed. We were very young when this happened, and of course, she needed someone to take care of us while she was having an operation. This was at a time where my mother and father were still together, or at least not divorced yet, and so, she passed the responsibility rightfully to our dad who was "meant" to take care of us. I don't have a clue why some men or women state they would like a child, but when it comes to the crunch and care and sacrifice for the child, he or she backs out and somehow can't do it or take the responsibility. This was what my dad did, for when he took us in he didn't have a clue what to do; therefore, he stupidly went to his mother to get advice. I'm not trying to say that parents can't get advice from their grandparents, but if the grandparents are anything like my grandmother, then I can stress it was the most stupid action to do. I was horrified to hear that my grandmother's advice was not providing the lessons of caring for a baby, nor to suggest that she would take care of us temporarily, but to take us to a care home and put us in there for a temporary period.

Any parent with common sense knows what a care home is and would not even think one second of doing that, especially when the mother and father are not dead and the mother is just having a small operation to have her tonsils removed. The reason why I have such a dislike for my grandma and father was because my grandma told him to do it and then my father followed it. They drove to a care home, about which I don't have a clue as to the area or its name now, and tried putting us in there. Fortunately, the social care people were professionals, and phoned up my mother to ask if she had decided to have me and my sister put into care. As you can quite imagine, my mother was distraught, and in the end my father got scolded not just by the Social Services, but by my mother, and looked stupid in front of the Social Services for even believing he could do that.

I know, deep inside the core of my mind, that my mother could never make up such a story, and carry on living in life, knowing that she lied. I even questioned my father about this event and his behaviour changed from a naturally cheerfulness to a hollow and wooden atmosphere, like guilt had slapped him straight in the face. On that day, we got into an argument, and after I knew it was true, the bond which we were meant to have just disappeared into thin air. He might be called "dad" because he created us, but when it comes to loving him and looking up to him, I only see him as a support for money rather than a support for my emotional needs. What has helped me move on is the statement I heard from an audio which was, "You came through your parents, and not from them." In the end, I belong to the God, source, universe and ultimate energy that made me. If my dad does not love me, then it does not matter because he did not make me, but I was gifted to my parents by God.

Back to the topic of school; everything at first was wonderful, my homework was done on time and my childhood was free of pain and stress. There was some small bullying like name calling but, apart from that, I ignored it. It was all fine until, at the age of six, I was moved to the mainstream school system

Analysis Thought: Chapter 2

This chapter was about how my home-schooling started and the unfortunate neglect which my father inflicted on me, followed by the heartless advice of a woman who's meant to be my grandmother. I would like to go over in this Analysis Thought how to deal with a parent, parents or family member if they are just as cruel and wicked as mine are. For those children who still have their mother and father together, I state deeply that it is good...

To be Grateful
Now, it's very rare to see to people to have loved each other for over five, ten, twenty-three, forty or even fifty years and for their children to experience the childhood of having at least two parents together with them, whether it was through good times of playing in the park, to tough times like when you get into arguments. If you're one of those people, just thank the Lord or whichever God you believe in your religion that your parents are in a happy marriage and still love each other to the fullest. Some people like me can cry the pain off and move on with having a single parent, while others without their mother or father, whether split up or one deceased, have crashed and burned mentally which also affected them psychologically. Just be thankful that you are blessed with them and

not had to go through the pain of experiencing a parental divorce.

Enjoy each minute

Sometimes not everything lasts forever in life. Your parents could be together forever, but also remember that people can change or that some things can end even if they are perfect. Enjoy each day of your parents' love for each other. If you do see a change, you can try to stop a divorce from happening but, if it does happen, don't blame yourself. It's not your fault and there are other reasons why the parents have decided to go their separate ways. I have known couples to be together for over twenty years before deciding they want to go their separate ways and it's 90/100 that it's not the child's fault for it. Appreciate and enjoy the time, for you never know when it could change. As for those whose parents are already divorced or are separating right now, know that firstly…

It's not your fault

A divorce is never pleasant and, because of the strain and suffering of it all, some children tend to blame it all on themselves. They think that, maybe they were trouble-makers, and made their parents' lives so hellish that they had enough. It also could be because the child thinks their disability has caused the divorce. I thought that too, but what I want to let the children of divorced parents know is: unless you tried to split them up or that you tried getting your parents to fight, that it's not your fault at all. The parents decided to go for their own reasons and the burden should not be all on you; if anything, none at all. Your parents wanted you because they loved you and they were with you even before any fights or signs of separation happened and, even if they split, they still will love you no matter what.

Be Strong

It is very beneficial to have a good cry; crying helps us rid stress chemicals in our body as well as keep the lens of our eyes clean, but what we must not do is end up crashing mentally. We, as the next generation of our forefathers, must cry, wipe away the tears, lift our head up high and keep going to achieve whatever goals we have. Through doing this, not only will you have strengthened your confidence and self-esteem, but also you can prove to both your parents how unique you are and how their sacrifice has not been in vain, prove to them that you are a special person and an achiever; for your happiness is all that your parents want. Once they see this, they know their mission of bringing you up has been accomplished.

I look at these four factors and do my best to keep them all. I feel grateful my parents decided to have me and be together until I was the age of two. I enjoyed every minute of playing with my father in the park and going on holiday with my mum before the pressure came on. I know is not my fault for my parents' divorce, it was their decision and it had nothing to do with my being the culprit.   The most important thing of all is, even when I cry my eyes out at night, I wake the next morning to smile, get up from my bed and move on because I know I'm unique and I can achieve whatever I set my mind to and one of my goals is to write this book and help others

Chapter 3: Bullying

Year 2000 arrived, and it was time to be moved from the cosy warm centre, into the mainstream school system. I remember the excitement that rose in me like butterflies, many thoughts whizzed around in my small imaginative head such as "I'm growing up, I can make more friends...or at least try to" and "I'll be learning new subjects". To be quite honest, the academic subjects were more exciting to me than the possibility of the new playground and what new foods I could have at school dinner.

After a wonderful Christmas, school started again. I remember that grand old day when I first stepped into the Year 2 classroom. It smelled of newly fresh books and pencils, chairs were neatly placed and everything towered over me like personified giants, expressing how big they were, by towering over my six-year-old physique. A wave of pride and happiness came over me and, for the first month in Year 2, everything was wonderful and joyful. I loved homework, school dinners tasted amazing and the playground was one big jungle waiting to be explored. In my imagination, I was prepared for any beasts and ferocious insects and creepy crawlies that could possibly spring out from any direction, but in all the excitement, the beast that I didn't know how to face was the bully. After a month, that's where my long, draining struggle surviving in school began.

Bullying

To treat in an intimidating manner. To force one's way aggressively or by intimidation. To inflict, or deal, physical, mental and psychological damage on the weak.

Bullying is one of the most straining and stressing times a child must go through when they're in school. Homework bothers you, teachers may annoy you, but bullying is something much deeper and inflicts the most pain and misery on to the victim. Bullying needs to be stopped or at least, if not stopped, then strongly punishable to the bully when or if caught at it. After the first month in school, the name calling got worse, possibly because there were more children bullying me in groups, and I didn't have any friends whatsoever. I only had one friend in school. She was sweet and kind, and I was even invited to her birthday party. That was the only space of time where I felt my troubles being lifted; then she moved to a new house and that killed any sort of joy I had for the next year and a half in school. I was mentally and physically beaten and I felt depression sink in my heart, until I felt like no-one could, or even would help me anymore.

The Different Types of Bullying

There are three main diverse types of bullying and, before going into my experience of bullying, I will address the three main ones which can really affect and damage a child.

- **Physical Bullying**

This can be such as beating, slapping, kicking or anything which can leave a mark or in the worst cases draws blood from the victim. Physical bullying is of course not pleasant at all. I remember those dreadful times in school, when I was trying to escape from children who used skipping ropes as whips to hurt me. I felt a lot worse after, because after school, I would see my mother's anxious face, as she spotted the bruises on my arms and face, and the constant poking and pinching which annoyed me in the extreme. Physical bullying in my opinion is easier to deal with than mental and psychological bullying. Yes, you get punched, slapped and hit, but the cuts and bruises do heal and fade. As for the other two types of bullying, they are much stronger and more subtlety damaging; plus the wounds result in either a total change of life and environment, or never heal at all. Other traits of physical bullying can be...

- Using objects to inflict harm (for me it was skipping ropes and rocks)

- Fighting (as in ganging up on one or more victims before they must fight to survive)

- Physical harming (pushing, kicking, pinching, spitting etc...)

Mental Bullying

Traits of mental bullying can be name-calling, manipulating and saying negative comments over and over, to bring down the victim's self-esteem and confidence. A bully, who bullies their victims mentally, will constantly torment their victim's mind, using every painful comment and remark to make the victim feel useless and worthless. A few statements that crush self-esteem can be...

- "Break from me and you won't have any friends."
- "Without me you will be all alone."
- "Do you really think you can do that? Don't be so stupid."
- "You're worthless, fat and useless" and so on.
- "If you don't do this (for example, maybe their homework) you will be in trouble."

These might not seem effective, if you have grown out of that and know what will get you into problems or not. However, sometimes this is what children, and even teenagers of today, must go through and this is from my experience. I can't stress enough that mentally damaging bullying is more harmful than physical; the comments and horrible experiences sink into your mind and construct themselves there until you're deeply sick.

My mental bullying came from a girl who lived in an orphanage. I will tell of her in the next chapter but, just to give background information, she was the worst bully of them all in school. She made me feel useless, depressed and feeling like I was not worth a penny. In school, since I had no proper friends, then she became my half-bully and half-friend because I could only hang around with her, but still I had to do what she told me. If I ever broke away, she would threaten that she would tell the teacher that I was being mean to her, or that I would be lonely. I could have told the teachers the truth, but again they were neglectful and this didn't help at all with the bullying either. The constant remarks and comments tormented me and brought me down to my lowest level. Sometimes I thought to myself that I wanted to die and never come back, nor wake up the next morning, because the constant loneliness at that age was unbearable.

- **Psychological Bullying**

Mental bullying is indeed harsh and stressing to the core, but psychological is when mental bullying is dealt with at a deeper level. Traits of this type of bullying can be blackmail, torture (physical or mental) and the worst effect of this type of bullying is that the victim's whole personality and future outcome can be changed forever, in this case for the worse. I'll give an example of the way psychological subjects can change someone's mind, attitude or mood. What happens when you watch psychological horror? Or when horror, of that sort, suddenly pops up on your TV screen? For people who like horror or getting scared, it won't be so scary, because they know of it and like it. However, for sensitive people like me, when a certain psychological horror pops up on TV, my whole body, attitude and mind changes, my heart beats fast, my mind becomes alert, my eyes water in fear and once I have switched off the TV, I curl up in bed shivering in fear, making sure I look around my surroundings and stay awake if possible.

I also suffered psychological bullying too. I felt emotionally damaged inside, and the fact that the teachers and elders, who should know better, didn't bother to help me, when I was explaining to them in tears that I was being bullied, was even worse for me.

They would reply with "Don't tell lies" and walk away to carry on their own business, or they would become cross and scold me like it was my fault that I was being bullied, or because to them it seemed I was saying the same lies all the time. I became so stressed and closed in, that I was even thinking of becoming a bully myself, just so I could be left alone and not be constantly bullied five days a week from 9:00am to 3:00pm. I didn't like it when I saw my mum's face frown, because she knew she had a lot to deal with, plus she did already so much for me and I didn't want to see her sad.

To keep her happy, I even made up stories of how good school was and all the great friends I had. In the end, near the time when I was taken out, I could not hide it from mum any longer because she noticed my side-effects of bullying which I shall explain later in this chapter. Now it's time to focus on the present and I shall explain how my memories of bullying had an impact on me by explaining my everyday experience of bullying.

Experience of Bullying: Part 1

To explain my experience of being bullied and how it affected me, I shall go over a typical school day of mine in which the possible situations and traits of bullying would occur.

- **Morning 06:00am – 09:00am**

It was 6am and the sky just started to brighten, showing its gentle shades of royal blue. Before the rush started, I was just settling in bed, and absorbing the quiet interior of my room. It was a very peaceful and therapeutic time; I always wished it lasted forever, that time would freeze and I would not have to think about bustling out of bed, eating breakfast, washing, dressing and finally getting on the bus which carried me to my childhood perception of hell. I was then wakened by the sound of my mother's voice, as she urged me to get up otherwise I would be late for the bus.

I really loathed waking each morning, knowing I had to go to that institution of pain and nightmare, which was meant to be a place of learning and enjoyment. I sometimes felt so scared about going to school that I would pretend I was sick or that I hurt myself badly, so that somehow I could not go to school. My mum thought I really did hurt myself sometimes, or that I was sick, and would not let me go to school; other times she thought

I was being naughty for no reason and would scold me, before getting me ready for school. There were times when I was so stressed about meeting with bullies in my school that I really did become sick. The stress of having to cope with the strain every day caused me physical pain such as...

- **Sickness:**

This meant throwing up or feeling sick so I could not move anywhere without feeling dizzy and weak. My mother thought that my immune system was low, which in any chance was due to the extreme amount of stress I felt in school. Therefore, she took care of me a lot in my childhood. I felt deeply sickened by the fact that even if I was being punched and kicked in school, no matter how much I cried, or tried to send help, everyone would just ignore me, even the adults and the teachers who would just cover it up and ignore me.

- **Stomach Pains:**

Bad abdominal or stomach pains, which really hurt me and left me in tears. I was not sure if it was from the physical poking or hitting by bullies, or from deep stress; all I knew was that the pain was killing me. An example of the impact of this pain happened once in the speech centre, when the pangs returned in my stomach. Therefore, I had to rest and then my mother had to be called because I looked pale. That really was the only time the teachers decided to help me, for it would have cost them greatly if they didn't do anything for me at that time. I fell asleep and when I woke I was greeted by my mother and taken home.

- **Eyebrow Plucking:**

Now I'm sure this one is quite interesting. Certain questions might arise such as, "What do you mean eyebrow plucking?" "How can eyebrow plucking be effective in a negative way?" I shall explain more of this in the next chapter but when I state eyebrow plucking, I don't mean the natural tweezers' plucking, It was stress and anger that made me start the habit of constantly plucking vast amounts of my eyebrow hair out and leaving me with only a few. This was one side-effect, which made my mother start to wonder what was going on in my school.

- **Weight Gain:**

Apart from the unhealthy school dinners we had every day causing me to put on weight, another stressing effect was a large amount of weight gain. The average weight for an eight-year-old child is 57.2 kilos which is 126 pounds. At the age of eight, I weighed 73.3 kilos which was 162 pounds. At that age, I was overweight, and it was so drastic that I had to be taken to a dietician, and find a solution to burn off the weight. The school dinners didn't help either, since all I remember having was fast food, for example, burgers, fries, chocolate, sweets and oily food. The vast consumption of these foods made me feel unhealthy and sick. I could not run as fast as I wanted and I was called even more names by children, such as "Fat" and "Lard". Altogether, my confidence vanished; I felt worthless and cold inside.

At 8:30am I would get on the school bus and sit by myself in the back seat while the other kids were picked up and enjoyed their conversations. I just wanted to crawl into the dark and stay there forever or at least until it was time to go home again. There were two bus drivers who drove us to the school every day, one man and one woman. I don't have a clue how either of these two people got a job, since they never liked me and the other children on the bus. I would get snapped at to be quiet because we became a little noisy or just because they were annoyed. Instead of feeling scared of them, I was angrier at them for their rudeness and unnecessary dislike towards me. I was somehow always targeted and received a snap or two from the woman whenever the woman was angry. It didn't help that I also had a weak bladder and could easily wet myself if I didn't get to a toilet on time. The terrible memories of the woman was when I had a small accident on the bus and had to somehow survive her wrath when she found out about it, either by my telling her or just by her realizing it when I got up from my chair. For me, it was an embarrassing experience and it lowered my determination to make more friends. I arrived at the school and, with a sigh of remorse or resentment, I would enter.

- **Morning: 09:00am-13:00pm**

The problems in the Year 2 classroom were not from the students but from the teachers whom I really feared back then. If I got something wrong, they would become angry without trying to understand me and thought I was just being a rebel for no reason. An example was when the Queen was going to be driven past an area near to the school in her car. What the students had to do was colour the UK flag so they could wave it in respect as she was driven past.

Sounds very simple like that, but then two questions arise; firstly, "What happens if the child does not know the colours of the flag?" and secondly, "What happens if they make a mistake?" For me, I had those two troubles and it made that day the worst one of my life.

I had never seen the UK flag before, nor known which colours it had, nor where the colours were meant to be placed. I was constantly barked at by teachers because I would colour the wrong area blue, red or white. Sometimes the colour would go over the lines and accidentally mark another colour. At my fifth attempt to colour the UK flag correctly, I remember the red accidentally marking the blue and my heart sinking in disappointment at myself. I really couldn't take another lecture from the beasts of hate so I hid my flag and followed the students and teachers to the road where the Queen would be driven by. I waited at the road and, as the teacher exclaimed to wave the flags, I waved mine fast and quickly so the teacher would not spot my mistake. The car drove past and, in a flash, it was all over. On my way home from that fateful day, I thought to myself as I pondered on that day, "What was the point of it?" "All that shouting and scolding just for an event which didn't take longer than a minute and I had to cope with that?"

I returned home more depressed and sad than I ever was before, I somehow knew that the teachers were not going to be easy or friendly to me, therefore things were going to grow harder.

- **Afternoon in the playground: 12:00pm-13:00pm.**

Back to my typical day of school: at 12:00pm it was time to enter the canteen. I know today that the school dinners were so unhealthy but still they tasted good. The canteen was a place of enjoyment where I could enjoy my time alone and escape the nightmare of it all for the next hour or until I hit the playground. Normal dinners in the school would be burgers, chips, hot dogs, pasta and many more. For the dessert, it would be jelly or chocolate cake or a really disgusting rice pudding which tasted of soggy rice grains in a milky sauce.

After I ate and rested my full tummy, I headed to the playground where I would enjoy my half hour playing if the experience was good, or try to play by myself and escape the school kids if the experience was bad. Ninety percent of my experience in the playground was unpleasant, because I was called names like Banana or I had objects thrown at me or used to hit me. The teachers would not always allow this to happen, but mostly this did happen when the teacher was not present in the playground. Therefore, I would mostly try to remain on my own by sitting on the bench or moving to a large oak tree which was far away on a hill in the playground. That was the only place where I had peace; I could lie underneath the large oak tree and watch the rays of light come though the branches and feel their warmth dance on my face. In that one spot, I could think about all the things I wanted to do and let out my tears without being spotted by stoical others who didn't care about me. Time always seemed to fly by fast in the playground; what felt like half an hour was five minutes to me and in no time the school bell would ring, alerting us to all come inside and attend to our lessons. The dread of school returned and I stood in a line with thirty other kids being counted by a teacher to check if any had run away. I did have multiple thoughts of trying to run away before, but the gate was locked and the top of the metal fence had pointy spikes so it would be pointless and painful for me if I tried to. With a deep sigh, I headed back to class in a line and awaited the nightmare that should happen to me next.

- **Afternoon Lessons: 13:00pm- 15:00pm**

Afternoon lessons would begin and, as I sat at the table with a few other students, my mind was not focused on my work. It was focused more on the time and longing for it to go faster. Not a lot of bullying happened in the afternoon lessons but I still got scolded by teachers if I got one question wrong or made a small mistake.

All in all, in the afternoon lessons I was more cautious about the teachers than the students picking on me.

Neglect from Teachers

I want to alert children, teenagers and adults alike about how teachers can be just as awful as the students, because, even though the teachers were not physically bullying me as the students did, the teachers at my school still did it mentally, by neglecting and ignoring my pleas and cries for help when I did finally tell them I was being bullied. Some of their attempts to neglect me would be...

None of the Teachers Would Listen to Me

This situation would happen often since I had some bullies and other students to cope with. Before I told the teachers, I would try my best to keep it to myself for fear of causing my mother trouble or just because I was afraid, but I must stress that it's never, ever, good to keep negative feelings and stress; for it can cause severe pain and misery, as I explained in the physical side-effects of bullying.

When I was at the end of my limit, I finally plucked up enough courage to tell a teacher that I was being bullied by students. All the teacher said was, "You have to toughen up, just ignore them and don't listen."

I then explained that I was being targeted by students who used the playground skipping ropes and other playground objects as tools to hurt me.

It was only then that the teacher told me she would sort it out but I still needed to "toughen up" and "ignore them".

Unfortunately I don't think the teacher's way of sorting the problem was effective because, when Monday arrived again and I was in the playground, I still got the physical beatings and toys thrown at me.

The Teachers Would Try to Cover it up

When I was in physical, emotional and psychological trauma in the mainstream school, the teachers would just ignore me and tried to cover it up. They kept telling my mother how I was fine and I was just over-reacting and being naughty for no reason. Fortunately, my mum knew better than to listen to their words. She aimed to find out what was wrong, through the mental effects of bullying which I was feeling at the time.

Mental Effects of Bullying

Throughout the period of bullying, my mental state and self-esteem were at a dangerously low point. I felt useless, I thought I was ugly, I thought I was a nuisance and should just disappear from the face of the earth. Therefore, these were the mental effects of bullying I felt in school.

- **Depression:**

Any unfortunate event can lead to a person feeling depression; therefore, from the time I entered the mainstream school, to the point where I was taken out, I was completely miserable and depressed. All I could see was doom and gloom, every day seemed a nightmare, and I just wished I could escape from the pain I felt every time I woke and knew I was going to school.

- **Loneliness:**

Along with the depression, I was very lonely at school. I didn't have anyone to talk to, therefore, I would only sit by myself in the playground, or sit alone in class, while other students talked with each other before lessons started. Loneliness is one of the most horrible emotions to feel for, when you have it, you always feel that you are locked in a dark room. When your lonely life seems lifeless and worthless, you are not sure what to do, how to be happy, and it seems that all the life has been sucked out of you.

- **Self-Harm:**

The biggest effect of mental bullying is the fact that you want to harm yourself, instead of wanting to harm others or even the bully that is tormenting you. Therefore, I inflicted self-harm by constantly plucking out my eyebrow hairs. After I was home-schooled and free from the trauma, I kept pondering and thinking about why I did it, why I would damage myself when others were harming me, why I let others harm me, etc. Unfortunately, even to this day, I cannot find the true reason for why I harmed myself.

However, the main reason I did this to myself was to show my mum, without my knowing it at that time, that I was not ok, and the situation and my well-being were becoming more serious.

- **Sleeping Problems:**

I was constantly tired, since going to school every day made me frightened and stay awake all night. Sometimes I didn't even want to sleep, because of the nightmares I would have about school were too frightening. Although I can't remember all my nightmares, I knew that they were affecting me badly, making me unable to function in the day, have black bags under my eyes and made my mum very concerned.

Analysis Thought: Chapter 3

Bullying Advice for Adults
In this Analysis Thought chapter, I want to give parents and other adults who don't yet have children, awareness of bullying, how they can notice the signs and how to sort it before it affects their child. Therefore, I shall do this by explaining the symptoms my mother saw in me when I was being constantly bullied.

What my Mother Observed
My mother started noticing signs of my bullying, after I went into Year 2 of the mainstream system. Some signs she started to observe were:

- **Depression:**

The first sign my mother noticed in me, when the mainstream bullying started, was that I was very low and depressed. I had no energy left in me whatsoever; all I wanted to do was return home from school, go to my room and stay in there for the rest of the day before going to sleep.

- **The Desperate Need to Come Home:**

The second sign was the fact that I always wanted to come home. I still remember the times when, each time I finished a school play, I would run to my mother afterwards and beg and cry to come home with her.

My mother saw I was not ok but didn't decide to take any action, since she thought it was just a phase I was going through and that things would clear up as I stayed longer at school. It was terrible when my tearful attempts to come home didn't work and she would walk home while I watched from the school window. The teachers didn't help either, since when I begged my mother to take me home, they would laugh, smile, and say I was being silly and I was just being sensitive and naughty for no reason. After my mother went home, they went back to their same cruel personalities and just made my life a misery by ignoring my bullying problems and scolding me for telling so-called "lies".

- **The Desperate Need to Avoid School:**

After all my attempts to come home failed, I became very scared about waking up in the morning, only to experience the same harsh, painful experiences again. Therefore, the third sign my mother saw was my throwing tantrums and making it extremely hard for her to get me on to the school bus. The bus drivers were also bullies and just didn't like children. If my mum could get me onto the bus to school, they would just be cold and snappy at me all the way there for no reason, or for reasons which were not called for.

For most of my journey on the school bus, I sat there quietly, sometimes even silently crying to myself, wondering why I was going through this hell in the first place. When I hear about some school kids bunking off school, in a way I can understand it, especially if they were getting this sort of treatment before they just stopped caring about their education.

- **Withdrawal Symptoms:**

The fourth sign my mother saw was my constant behaviour, being withdrawn and anti-social to everyone. I can't fully explain why I decided this, but I just didn't want to be around anyone any more. Children seemed to scare me, and all I wanted to do was stay close to my mum. After home-schooling started, my mother could slowly show me that not all children were bullies and teach me how to socialize with people.

- **Illness:**

This was the fifth sign my mother acted upon. She realized I was becoming unnaturally ill, which resulted in me having dizziness, nausea and throwing up. When she went to the school to find the reason why I was so ill, the teachers stated that they didn't know the reason, and that it was best I should check with a doctor. Luckily my mother did, and she found the cause to be extreme educational stress; however, this was after I inflicted self-harm.

- **Urinary Problems:**

Along with every other problem I had, including the fact that I had to cope with bullying, loneliness and the negative attention I got from having Mild Autism, I suffered extreme urinary problems. My mother noticed that I was wetting my bedcover a lot more than usual, and the problem was not clearing up. Since wetting the bed constantly is not a clear sign of bullying, the sign was not strong enough, in my mother's eyes at that time, to be addressed. The experience of constant unitary problems was terrible, since I not only did it at home, but it would happen on the school bus as I was being driven up to the school. As you can figure out, the bus drivers were distraught with rage when I had to tell them quietly that I had an accident, since they thought I was doing it on purpose and had a really disgusting habit.

- **Self-Harm:**

The seventh and final sign made my mother realize that the bullying and problems had not cleared up. As I'll explain in the next chapter, my mother noticed my pain through the constant eyebrow plucking. After some research, I found this illness to be called Trichotillomania, a condition caused by stress and anxiety, where the person keeps plucking out their eye lashes, or eyebrows, until noticeable hair loss is seen by the victim or others.

What can Adults do to stop the Bullying of their Child?

There are a few solutions to the bullying; however, these solutions are for a mild level of bullying and would not help a child that is being heavily bullied. I shall explain the solutions for a child who has mild bullying, explain why they could not work for extreme bullying and explain my mother's solutions for dealing with the bullying.

Types of Bullying

There are two types of bullying. These types are:

- Mild Bullying: where the situation, once handled, is sorted and the bullying of the child dies down quickly.

- Extreme Bullying: where mild solutions for the bullying won't deal with serious and more damaging situations for the child who is being bullied. This can result in the child having the same, or even worse, effects that I have explained in this chapter.

Solutions for Mild Bullying

Mild bullying, in my opinion, is when the bullying gets addressed. Therefore, this either means that the bullying stops fully, or becomes less serious than before, to the point where the child can, or in some cases will, cope with the bullying. When I explain 'can' or 'will', my measure of this is: when I'm in college with students, who can have rude tendencies, but do not cause me to have the extreme side-effects of bullying. Therefore, this means I can ignore them and continue with my own education. Things some adults will do to deal with mild bullying are:

- Tell their child how to deal with the bullies.
- Go up to the school's Headteacher.
- Address the bully's parents.
- Talk with the class teachers about the bullying.
- Ask if you may observe your child for one day in that environment. This will see if there is any real bullying going on, as well as test out if the teachers have anything to hide. If they refuse you permission to observe your child, then it is a sign that they have something to hide and they don't want you to know about it.

Why Some of these Mild Solutions won't work for Extreme Bullying?

In my opinion, although these solutions are very good and can help stop bullying, they would not be useful in the cases of extreme bullying; for example, such as the physical, mental and psychological bullying explained above in this chapter. The reasons why I believe these solutions would not have helped me with my situation are explained below:

• It's good to teach your child how to deal with bullies, for example, ignoring them, avoiding them, or just pretending that it's not bullying. However, even if a child uses these methods to deal with the experience of bullying, the bully themselves can be ten times harder to avoid; plus, they might also know what the child is trying to do and continue to make their school life worse just for their pleasure, reputation-building in the school or ego.

• I'm sure, in many cases, addressing the headteacher of the school has worked to cut a few bullying situations. However, this solution would have been fruitless.

If the neglect and bullying from teachers wasn't hard enough to deal with, I also had to deal with a headteacher who didn't seem to like me either. Therefore, the headteacher was the main culprit who lied to my mother, scolded me for trying to get help and made the situation even harder for me at school.

• This solution is also one of the main ones which can cut down a bully; however, in some cases, it doesn't. The probability of the bullying stopping, by addressing the problems with the bullies' parents, depends on their views and if they would care enough to tackle their son or daughter about it when they return home. For me, this could have been a possible solution; however, since my teachers ignored my explanations, the parents would, of course, have not known about their child bullying others.

• My mother did go to school to ask the teachers the reasons I was so ill and suffering so many unusual effects. Unfortunately, the teachers' lies gave my mum fruitless results and ended with me having to cope with extreme bullying for three years.

With all my reasons explained why mild solutions for bullying would not cure extreme bullying, my advice for adults on bullying is:

• Don't ignore your child's suffering: This advice can seem obvious; however, I have noticed one example of family members who ignore a situation where their son is practically being manipulated and controlled by a bully in front of everyone.

It might seem easy for some adults to ignore their child's bullying; however, this causes destructive effects for the child when they're older. For example, after the beginning of my third year in school, I thought everyone, including my mother, had ignored me. Therefore, I was deciding to become a bully myself and torment others just so I would not be bullied. From this, I found out the reasons why some children become bullies, and how the neglect of a parent can be so painful to them and to me. My father's neglect didn't help either, since after the divorce he only came once a week on Sunday, and never came to any school event or meeting to discuss the effects of my bullying.

• Get the police involved: This should only be done if the child returns home with serious bruising or injuries, which have the highest probability of arriving from their school environment, or receiving threats from bullying which can be life, mentally and psychologically threatening to the child. For some bullies, the force of the law will make them afraid and put them in their place. However, for some other bullies, this will cause more danger to the child. It's very wise that, if you do get the police involved in the case of your child's bullying, that the bullies themselves do not find out which child or parents have reported them.

- **Change schools:**

I would not highly recommend this advice, unless it is a last resort. Not only can changing schools be a difficult, and sometimes even financially demanding task but, for the child, it can make them feel more isolated and unable to cope with the next bully that would be in the new school.

- Take your child into home-schooling: For a lot of parents, this solution can be very difficult and complex. The reasons for this are that some parents would not know how to educate their child; they might not know where to find support for home-school children, they might not be able to cope with their child's problems or social issues, or the parents will maybe think it's illegal to take a child out of the mainstream system. In Chapter Five of this book, I shall explain the resources my mother found which were able to help her feel more secure and prepared to take me out of the mainstream and home-school me and, later, my elder sister. Home-schooling is not for everyone but, for those who decide this, you should be informed that it's not illegal and that it can be done whether you are a single parent or not. With all the solutions explained, it's time to move to Chapter Four.

Chapter 4: My Bully

Experience of Bullying: Part 2 My School Bully. This chapter is the final instalment of my time in school, before I was finally taken out of it by my mother. However, before we go into the story of how I was finally taken out of school, I feel it's important to explain the bully I had. Not only this will help you recognize the subtle symptoms of bulling, but it will also help you to know what to do and how to combat it.

My Bully: Foe or Friend?

My bully was a very complex person; therefore, the way to explain my bully was that she was both a bully and friend. As I told you before, I didn't have any friends at school, therefore, I realize now how the bully was easily able to come in and manipulate me easily, so I would not go and tell the teachers about her.

Who was my School Bully?

I remember that the bully lived in a care home, since she needed to be picked up to be taken to school. She might have had a difficult past to cope with, but even now I still don't accept that she took what could have been dreadful pain and stress out on other students including me.

Signs of Bullying

In what ways did she bully me?

Mental and Psychological Bullying and Their Symptoms

As I explained in the last chapter, there are three types of bullying: Physical, Mental and Psychological. The main two areas my bully/bad friend used on me were Mental and Psychological; therefore, she was a possessor and manipulator. Even though I am now an assertive person who cannot be manipulated, I understand why I accepted her as a friend during that period and still coped with her bullying. The reasons were:

- I was at my lowest ebb of self-confidence and esteem: Low confidence or self-esteem is the biggest killer of your wellbeing and outlook on life. The main reason why I accepted my bully as a friend, and accepted her cruel ways of bullying, was because I lost hope and had no confidence whatsoever. I felt like I was worthless and deserved the treatment I was getting, when I subconsciously knew that it was not true. When I was friends with this bully, I used to cope with it, since I thought that if I tried breaking friendship with her, I was being ungrateful and taking any friendship for granted.

- The bully didn't hit me: As I stated before, Mental/Psychological bullying hits harder and affects the victim's mind more than physical bullying, therefore, you don't have to punch or hit someone to become a bully or control your victim.

- Neglect from teachers: The worst part of having a bully/bad friend was that the teachers ignored me even when they knew this bad friend of mine was a bully. I remember once telling my mainstream teacher about the bully and her bullying, only to be scolded and told not to tell fibs. Once I realized the teachers were not going to help me, I thought my chances of escaping school were zero to none. Therefore, I gave up on life, making friends and, in the lowest cases, wished that I would die. An example of how the teachers would ignore the bullying was when I was playing with my school bully, and I had a plan to try and run away from her as soon as she was not looking.

As a seven-year-old child, I was a very fast runner, therefore, when this bully/bad friend and I decided to play the game "It", I ran as fast as my feet would carry me. It was working, until the point where the bully started to cry crocodile tears just because she couldn't catch up with me. What made it even worse was that one the teachers came to find what was wrong, and the girl was crying and stating how I was being mean to her and how mean, cruel and heartless I was being. Knowing that if I didn't return, I would get into trouble with the teachers, as well as the possibility of detention, I had to come back and apologize out of fear, just so I would get yelled at or told off by the teacher. When the teacher thought everything was ok and went back to her business, my bully gave me the most malicious and evil smile. As soon as I saw it, I did not only know I was in trouble, but I was also mad with rage at the teacher for treating me like this and letting me be harmed inside the school.

• I had no friends: Maybe if I had a friend, apart from this bully acting like one, maybe they would have defended me and helped me to get my confidence back to face the bully. However, since I was constantly called names, and hit with skipping ropes from every child in my school and classroom, the chance of making even one friend was non-existent. I did have one friend before she moved; however, the situation with the bully/bad friend happened after my loyal friend moved to a new house and changed schools.

Symptoms of Mental/ Psychological Bullying from my Bully

The main systems of bullying I got from my bully/bad friend; were:

• Threats of getting me into detention: As a child, we were taught that misbehaving children went into detention. As my Receptive Disorder always made me ten times more sensitive to the meanings of statements than other people, I was afraid of detention. I dreaded what would happen if I did get into detention, my mother's reaction to it after all the stress and challenging work she was being put though, and how much shame it would bring to her and our family for having a troublemaker in the family.

• Using my personal issues as a weapon: Only a few weeks back, my sister and I were having a verbal disagreement, therefore, she decided to use my present social issues as a weapon by stating, "You have social issues and therefore you haven't made any loyal friends till even now". After that sudden painful reminder about my present social situation, and how I have had this ever since childhood school, I went to my room and had to cool down for an hour and a half. If I didn't do this, the rage of hate and anger in me would have taken over and caused me to hit my sister. My school bully used the same methods of mental and psychological bullying on me, however, the only difference was that I didn't fill up with rage straight after, but instead came home and either cried to my mother about it, or went to my room and stayed in there for the rest of the day. Some personal remarks my bully/bad friend used on me were:

- "You won't get any friends." (She would use personal issues as the reason I could not get any friends. For example, I was too fat, disliked, ugly and everyone knew I had a disability, therefore, that's why I would not find a friend.)

- If you try breaking friends with me (or defend myself against her) I would go and tell the teachers." (Since the teachers seemed to believe everything the bully stated, and somehow didn't want to deal with my problems, the threat at that time was scary to me, since I would also get detention from teachers if the bully told them about me if I tried to run from her or escape.)

Effects of Bullying

Suicide: Suicide can affect anybody, whether that is a child, teenager or adult; however, what scares me the most was that I thought about what it would be like to join God at the age of seven. As I came back home and sat in my darkened room, all I thought was about how useless I was and how I didn't want to feel and be like this anymore. I was even close to suicide once; since when I was being taking care for by my grandmother on my father's side, and she was out of the kitchen, I would climb onto the counter, open the medicine cabinet and drink substantial amounts of various medicines for different illnesses. Another close call to death was when I was so depressed, that I saw bleach in the bathroom, and poured out a capful size to drink. Luckily, something in my subconscious stopped me from making this harrowing decision, since if I carried out my plan, I would not be here to write this book and help others in similar situations to mine.

The reason that stopped me drinking this bleach was something in my mind telling me to "keep on fighting" and "wait a little longer". I was not sure why waiting longer would help, but this sudden thought saved my life, since I didn't drink the bleach and came out of the bathroom.

The Worst Social Event of my Life

The worst social event of my life; was when my elder sister and I were invited to the birthday party of one of my school students. This birthday party was being held by the student's parents at their house, therefore, even though I didn't know these people well, I still wanted to go and have fun at a birthday party. Normally, birthday parties should not be the place where you experience your worst social event in childhood. However, for me it was so and it all began when my sister and I came into the student's house to enjoy their birthday party.

The Problems at the Party Began

I knew as soon as I entered the house that I was going to have trouble with the girls at the party, since somehow, they kept on going off in their groups, and whenever I tried to join in, the leader of the pack would treat me like rubbish and push me back out again. Even worse, the mother of the student that invited me didn't like me at all; therefore, she was rude, mean and disrespectful to me as a person. Before the mother of the student showed her shallow side, the only solution left was to hang around with the boys. However, reasonably, they didn't want one girl in their group, so I was left alone in the house to wonder and watch all the kids playing with each other at a distance. This was completely normal for me at that time; however, for my sister it was a shock, since she didn't know until this birthday party that I was being treated this way by students in school.

I remember my sister sitting on the sofa crying for me, and when I asked if she was alright, the mother snarled and said that I was ruining the birthday party for her; therefore, this was why she was crying. Since I didn't understand the true reason why my sister was crying, I thought it was true, decided to move away from all social contact and stay by myself away from everyone. This was the time where things got worse for me and my sister, since my sister went to the leader of the girls' group and questioned her about why I was being pushed out of their group. Unfortunately, the leader of the girls' group was the birthday student's sister, which meant my sister and the girl got into a verbal fight, after which, the mother of the girl decided to lock me and my sister outside the house in the back garden.

Cruel Treatment from Parent

As I stated, the mother of the lead girl decided to lock me and my sister out of the house, in the back garden, because she thought my sister and I wanted to cause trouble for pleasure or for no apparent reason. Although my sister told me it was not my fault we were in this situation, my heart was panged with pain and I wished I hadn't come, didn't exist and didn't make my sister a recluse from the children inside the house. After an hour or so of sitting on the stone pavement in the back garden for an hour, the mother decided to open the door and let us back in, while she called our mother to take us both home. It was fine with me, since I was almost in tears and wanted to go home; however, my sister would not go home without a good verbal fight. She argued with the mother, telling her that how she treated me was wrong and that she would tell our mum about this once she arrived.

This caused the mother to be in so much rage that, when another mother came to pick up her child from the party, she asked if the mother could take me and sister home with them. To this day I'm still horrified how she had responsibility for all the kids at the party, and yet when something went wrong, she would risk our lives by giving us over to a stranger who didn't know us whatsoever. Plus, it must have put stress on the other mother, who was not expecting this.

Luckily, we didn't go with the other mother; we demanded that we sit there on the carpet floor until our mother came to pick us up. Once my mother had come to the house to pick us up, all I remember is screaming and crying while wanting to tear the student's mother to pieces.

The house was on a busy street, so many people looked with fear and wonder at how and why I was reacting like this, while the mother was embarrassed and said how I was ruining the party for everyone. To this day my sister and I, as well as my mother, know that we - the two of us - were rejected and disrespected at the party by the kids and the parent of the birthday student. After my sister told out mum about the terrible situation, she swore she would not take me to any of the school students' parties again, and to be quite honest, I never wanted to go to one again either.

Experience of Bullying from Teachers and Adults

My Worst day in School
Every child in a school can typically have a worst day. They might fail their maths exam, they could lose their best friend, or in the worst cases, be told that they have been excluded from the school. However, on top of the bullying and neglect, the worst day I had in school was when I almost got into detention for something I did not do. When I think back to that moment of the worst day, I still get shivers and even cry at times, due to the pain and shock I felt while in it. My worst experience went as follows:

I was playing in my classroom by myself, unaware of the other school kids playing together. Suddenly the headteacher of the school, followed by my school bus driver, came into the classroom in a frantic rage and demanded that I come to her. Since I was afraid and unsure about what I did, I came over and was prepared to hear what I could have possibly done wrong. What came from the headteacher's mouth was shocking, since she said that I was being put into detention, since I swore at the bus driver on the way to the school. At this age, I was seven-eight years old, and never even knew the first letter of any swear word, therefore, I tried to say something to defend myself; however, the teacher told me to be quiet and listen to her.

Not only was the headteacher's body language intimidating, and her voice was loud and painful in my ear drums, but I also had to feel the embarrassment of all the school kids looking at me and the situation in shock; also, some were even laughing at the situation. To this day, I'll never forgive the bus driver who framed me, for she had no proof whatsoever that I swore at her, plus there were several other kids on the school bus who could have easily uttered a swear word behind her back. Therefore, why weren't all the school kids ordered to the headteacher, and why was I the only one being called and told off instead?

After the headteacher's disheartening scolding, threats of detention, and after she went off to her chores, the school driver just smiled and followed behind her, as if she had won some type of imaginary war against me. I went back to my spot feeling more than sad and angry; I was in an elevated level of shock and anxiety. As I was driven home by those bus drivers, all the school kids asked if I was ok on the bus as I didn't say a word and was holding back the tears that were forcing themselves around my eyes. All the woman did was tell the other kids to leave me alone, since I was naughty and deserved what I got.

When I returned home and my mother saw me, she realized from the second she looked at me that something terrible had happened. Therefore, I ran to my mum and burst into tears as I told her about my worst day, what I was accused of, followed by the bad report written about me. The day after that incident, my mum was called by the school's headteacher to explain whether I had heard any offensive/swearing language from her. My mother was shocked and angry and therefore she explained that she never would use such language around me.

As you can see, this would be the straw that broke the camel's back, since on top of this I had to cope with being bullied for having atypical Autism, Receptive and Expressive Language Disorder, social problems and only having a bully as a friend. This was the main reason why I contemplated suicide at the age of seven, since I believed I was forever going to be in hell and feel constant pain.

Final Stages of Schooling

After three long and painful years in school, it seemed that God saw my suffering, and therefore, decided to answer my prayers. I can't help thinking that it was God also who came into my subconscious to tell me not to kill myself, as I was contemplating suicide in the bathroom. The reason why this section is called the final stages was because my mother finally saw the ugly side of the school in the flesh, and realized that, if I didn't come out of school soon, my life, wellbeing and personality would be permanently distorted or destroyed. In my opinion, if my mum had left me in that school any longer, I would have committed suicide without hesitation.

Educational Stress

There are many types of educational stress, for example, a student can feel stressed about their exams. However, for me this was not about exams or homework; what caused my educational stress was the constant six hours of bullying. My mother's aim was not initially to get a letter claiming educational stress, however, when she saw the effects of bullying taking me over, she decided to take me to a doctor.

Therefore, when my mum took me to the doctor, the doctor realized that the effects were being caused by extreme bullying. As I explained before, the constant bullying caused me to start plucking out my eyebrow hairs for no reason at all. Therefore, my mum saw the signs of extreme bullying, as most of my eyebrow hair was gone, and I had small and sore patches around the eyebrow area where the eyebrow hairs should have been. This physical/psychological effect followed by the urinary problems, depression, constant crying and the suicide attempt made my mum realize something was seriously wrong, and take me to the doctor's. When my mum realized I was suffering educational stress, she wrote a letter to the school to address them about it. Through this letter, the teachers at the school realized that my mum was aware of my stresses, bullying and their side-effects in school. Therefore, this warned them that, that if nothing changed, I would be taken out from school.

Abusive Teacher
As stated above, there was a teacher in my school who was not fond of me and seemed to have

despised me. Therefore, on the day my mother came into the school, and witnessed her actions, that was the final straw for my mum. It made my mum decide to take me out of school and home-school me. The reason my mother came up to the school was to check on me and what happened in the classroom while I was there. Fortunately, I wasn't bullied on that day, since all the teachers and students seemed to leave me alone and didn't want to bother me. Despite this, my mother still saw the fact that I always was on my own, as well as the fact that I was quiet most of the time. Finally, when it was my mother's time to go home, I ran to her and begged her to take me home with her. Unfortunately, this teacher, who caused my mum fury, came up to us, and tried to make out everything was fine, every day was like this in the classroom, and I was being naughty and telling fibs for no reason.

She even tried to call me back into the classroom with her sickly-sweet voice; however, I was not a fool to fall for that.

I remember that day hiding behind my mother's legs as the abusive teacher came forward. Therefore, I knew her true colours, I was tired of being tormented by her and I absolutely refused to let my mother go home without me. After the abusive teacher finished telling lies, and my mum became suspicious, another teacher came over to my mum to talk about the situation. Therefore, while my mother was distracted with the second teacher, the first teacher attempted to get me back into class by grabbing my wrist and dragging me back in.

I screamed by the biggest scream I could ever do and started to cry as I drew my hand back from her grasp and held my mum's legs even more tightly. Unfortunately for this abusive teacher, she knew she was caught and could not hide her true colours any longer. My mum was literally filled with rage and anger. My mum's cheeks were red, her eyes glinted like glass, and, after a few seconds, she was telling off both teachers with such dominating force, that even I was afraid of her.

After my mother scolded both teachers, as well as announcing she was going to the headteacher about this, she picked me up and took me with her out of the school while all the time I was asking my mum if I had done something wrong. She replied "No", and stated how happy she was that I had made a noise instead of allowing that teacher to treat me that way. This was the final straw for my mother; she realized I wasn't getting a proper education there, and that I needed a place to grow on my own and build a foundation naturally. She realized that my bullying situation was not mild, and it had been causing all the eyebrow plucking, crying, depression and withdrawal symptoms. Therefore, my mother went to the headteacher the next day to declare that she was taking me out of school and would home-school me.

This chapter finally ends one of the toughest parts of my life; unfortunately, this was my childhood. After three long years of torment, the three types of bullying, almost becoming a bully and the point where I almost committed suicide, I was finally free from it all. I can't explain the feeling I had when my mother asked how I felt about not going back to school. I felt ecstatic, wired, happy and joyful. I was definitely ready to face home-school, no matter how many benefits and flaws it contained. God had finally answered my prayers and to this day I'm so grateful for that. Therefore, this finishes Chapter 4 and now on to Chapter 5 which is where the story of my home-schooling begins.

Analysis Thought:

Chapter 4
Bullying Advice for Children

From experience, I definitely know how hard, terrible and upsetting it is to experience bullying day in and day out, without any solution as to how, or when, it will cease. Therefore, in this analysis section, I want to give children, whether they are being bullied or not, advice on how to cope with it, avoid it and escape from it. I would like to give you advice on how deal with bullying.

How can I Deal with Bullying?

Dealing with bullying does not have an easy solution to the problem, however, learning how to deal with it can help you, or your child, avoid any further pain or stop them from self-harm or suicide. The advice I give to children, on how they can deal with their own situations of bullying is:

- **Find a place to be on your own:**

The playground at school was not the best place for me, since I got called names, hit with skipping ropes, pushed over, and just was humiliated and embarrassed by how everyone treated me. Therefore, one of my solutions to that problem was to head up a hill, which led to another playground, and sit behind a large oak tree which was located on the highest point of the hill.

Once I was there, I didn't have to think about other school kids finding me and tormenting me. Therefore, I spent all my playground time relaxing, releasing my stressful tears and finding my inner peace behind that large oak tree. Not all schools will have oak trees, therefore, what I advise is to try and find a haven to avoid the possible bullies who are in a given area. It could be in the classroom, around another group of kids who are not bullies, or even another part of the playground, but just make sure to find a haven where you can hide and not be spotted easily. The oak tree wasn't always the best hiding spot for me, since some school kids found me up there and I had to move either because of their bullying or just because I was fearful of them. However, much of the time was spent behind that oak tree, and nine times out of ten I wasn't discovered by others.

- **Talk to your parent/parents about it:** For me, I only had my mother to talk to about my pains and problems; however, the fact that she was there to listen to me and support me was the best gift I could ever get as a child.

It's never good to bottle your feelings up, since if you do, this can create stress, tension, depression and physical effects in your body, as well as illness and even suicide. That's why it's very important to find someone to talk to about your bullying, whether it's your parent, parents, grandparents, aunties, uncles, cousins, etc.

- **Tell your teachers about the bullying:**

Unfortunately for me, this was not one of my solutions for dealing with bullying. However, this does not mean that all teachers will ignore a student who tells them that they are being bullied. What I advise is: if one teacher ignores your bullying situation, don't keep quiet about it, keep on telling more teachers. What I believe is that, if a person makes enough noise for long enough, it will become an issue and will be unable to be ignored. Therefore, teachers with any sense will sort the situation, whether to keep the reputation of the school good, or they will do it because they care. Whatever the results, making enough noise will mean a good outcome for you.

- **Pray:**

I do understand that not all children believe in the Christian God, therefore, whether your religion is Christen, Muslim, or any other religion, I believe that the power of prayer helps in the long run. For me, as a child, the power of prayer helped me to find my inner peace and not go insane with the stressful life of bullying. As I was about to drink bleach from the cap in the bathroom, I was praying to God to forgive me for doing this and explained the reason why I felt I needed to do it at that time. Luckily, I heard the voice which told me to stop and it saved my life. I used to also listen to the Bible on cassette during my three years of bullying; therefore, as I laid on my pillow to listen to the stories of Jesus, I began to relax and feel the pain wash off me.   If you are an atheist, or do not believe in a God at all, I only hope that the subconscious inside you helps to combat your negative experiences of bullying and stop you from thinking about suicide or self-harm.

- **Don't become the bully:**

This solution to dealing with bullying is the most important one; however, it's easier to say it than to do it. When I thought about how I almost became a bully myself, I realized that the reason I was heading to becoming a bully was because I felt trapped with two negative choices. I could either become a bully and protect myself but unfortunately harm and torment others in the process, or I could not be a bully but still endure all the pain and stress I was going through.

What stopped me from Becoming a Bully?

The reason that stopped me from becoming a bully, just like my bully, was that I didn't feel pleasure, strength or happiness from making someone else insecure and sad. An example of this was the first and only time I decided to bully someone. This student was a very gentle, quiet, but happy boy who never was bullied and certainly didn't deserve it. Unfortunately, seeing that bullying was the only solution to protecting me from other bullies, I waited in my bus seat as he got on and made a rude comment about the coat he was wearing. I can't remember what comment it was, however, I still remember it being offensive since he started to cry afterwards.

As you can guess, a few seconds after he was crying, the bus driver came up to him and asked what was wrong. This is where fear struck into my heart, and I knew I was not a bully at all; let alone getting scolded by the driver in front of everyone, therefore, I quickly apologized to the boy afterwards and sat alone in my seat to reflect on the mistake I had made. From this experience, I realize now that bullies are just like me. Therefore, even though they seem tough and hard-shelled, they are really scared little kids inside, who could have gone through the experiences I was having at the time, and decided to become a bully themselves just so they would be left alone. I still do realize though that there are bullies who just do this for no reason. However, the next time you see or get a lashing from your bully, remember that they can also be just weak, timid, and scared and they decided to become a bully to solve their problems.

- **Tell your bully the truth:**

When I state this, I don't mean go over and be the first one to hit him or her since you will get into trouble. What I mean by this, is that if you have built enough courage to stand up to your bully, then this means the next time you see them, you tell them how they are, how what they're doing is unacceptable and that they are just weak in themselves. I really don't see how you can get into trouble just by verbally bashing them, unless you use racist or personalized comments about them. If none of those comments is used, you should not be put into detention for that. Running away from my bully in the playground may have almost got me into trouble; it was also a way of showing her that, at that point, I was strong enough to move away and show her up to be an absolute cry-baby.

- **Don't give up:**

This doesn't only go for school, but also goes for anything else in this world and your future goals. Therefore, in the case of bullying, the strongest advice I want to give to children and teenagers out there is to never give in or give up on yourself. Giving up seems an easier and quicker option for dealing with bullying, however, it will damage you in the long run. If I kept quiet when the teachers stated I told lies, I never would have got out of school. If I became a bully; I would have perhaps survived more easily in school, but my personality, mental wellbeing and psychological wellbeing would have been damaged ten times more.

If I gave up completely on ever reaching for help, I know I would either have become a troublesome child to my mother, or would not be on this earth any longer; since I wanted to leave the planet more than hope for a new future.

Chapter 5
Home-schooling Begins

Finally, after three years of pain, upset, torture and thoughts of suicide, I was free from it all through my mother taking me out and home-schooling me. I still remember the day when my mother asked how I felt about not going to school, but working from home instead. I leaped at the chance like fire to paper, and I never looked back nor regretted home-school afterwards. Home-school gave me the foundation to grow naturally and freely, while state schooling threw me in all directions like a puppet, while they still expected me to find the foundation myself. Home-school, also known as Education Otherwise, gave me the freedom to find myself spiritually, physically, mentally and emotionally, and I'm so thankful for that, since home- school gave me the power to set others free from the tortures of state school by writing this book.

What is Home-School/Education Otherwise?

Home-schooling, or Education Otherwise, is an alternative learning environment for children outside of state or private school. Not all parents are able or will be prepared to take their child out of school, since their child might love to be in their state or private school.

However, the other reasons why not all parents are able or prepared to home-school their child is because there will be many trials, tribulations and stress along the way, as a result of making your child better than the state-school system. Therefore, this is only for parents who are physically, mentally and psychologically ready to fight for their children's education and future, as my mum was, and still is doing today.

Where did Home-Schooling/ Education Otherwise Begin?

To find out the exact origin of home-school, it would take a lot of research into history. People such as Leonardo da Vinci were home-schooled; hence, this was well-established by the 15th century. It's also true that home-school was present before state schools were even formed.

Types of Home-schooling

Everyone might think that home-school is one type of education only; however, even though it's a unique kind of education, it does not have just one type of education. Home-schooling is a type of education with many distinct kinds. Therefore, you can imagine home-schooling at the core of the tree, with its many various kinds as the branches and leaves.

From my research into the subject, I found that such diverse types of home-schooling are:

- **Structured Home-school Learning:**
Structured home-schooling would also be described as school-at-home learning. Therefore, this means that the home-schooled child will have the most important subjects of school lessons taught to them, then a break, followed by more lessons until they are finished for the day. For me, being home-schooled at home gave me the same experience as going to a state school to be taught the academic subjects which create our life and world. However, the difference was that I could learn at my own pace, without being pressured and scolded by teachers who made out that making any mistake was unacceptable and should be punished. The main subjects I learnt at home-school were Maths, English Literature, English Language, Speed Reading, Speed Writing, English Writing, Essay Writing and Biology, followed by French.

- **Autonomous Learning:**
This type of education is from a school of education which encourages its students to be accountable for their own education and learning space. This body of home-school education helps their students find these by helping them to create self-awareness, the mindset to achieve and the freedom to speak

and discuss, which help them to learn for themselves through home-schooling, although I wasn't in an educational body with teachers encouraging me, I was still able to get enough support and guidance from my mother to learn by myself and do independent learning.

- **Afro-centric Home-schooling:**

Not very well known; however, this is where the child is taken out of school to learn their ancestral history, values and culture, as well as other home-school academic subjects. This type of home-school is done by ethnic minorities.

- **Unschooling/Natural Learning:**

This type of schooling encourages children to learn about life naturally, for example, children would learn through household responsibilities, natural life experiences and even playing games.

- **De-schooling/No Schooling:**

Unfortunately, this type of home-schooling is not a positive example of home-school, since it describes the type of people who take their children out of school but don't teach them anything whatsoever. Therefore, this means that they can stay at home and do whatever they wish, which means they're not getting the academic education they need.

From my research, I found that parents who fall into this category will teach their child basic English, Maths and Science, therefore, they would only be told those basics and nothing else about independent learning or deeper studies into these subjects for GCSE or IGCSE exams. Although it was not my mother's way of teaching us, she always said that everybody has a choice and you cannot make other people's choices for them.

There are many more types of home-schooling, hence, the ones shown here are a few types of home- schooling known to society, or for people who seek to learn about it.

Types of Home-schooling Methods

Along with the types of home-schooling, there are also different methods of home-schooling. Some different home-school methods are:

- **Classic Home-school Method:**

The first method is when the home-schooled student is taught the fundamentals of education in the classic method which help the child's overall development. For example, such subjects they would learn are Maths, English, Science, History, Philosophy and another language, etc.

- **Delayed Home-school Method:**

With the second method, children do not start to learn the fundamental subjects which contribute to their development until the age of eight onwards.

- **Unschooling Home-school Method:**

Based on the teachings and principles of John Halt, this method allows the home-schooled child to choose their path and make their own choices in the subjects they want to learn. There is a lot of criticism about this, since people think the child won't choose the right subjects needed, or will be less smart. However, great minds have been developed because they went through this type of home-school method.

Montessori Home-School Method:

Created by Dr. Maria Montessori, whose aim was to show adults that children can still be taught the important subjects they need for overall development in a free, but well-structured environment. Therefore, the Montessori home-school classroom would usually contain materials, and resources. This helps with the home-school students' sensory and motor training, and overall helps most of them to become 'explorers'. Parents of these types of home-school students would encourage them on their journey.

- **Eclectic Home-school Method:**
In this method, the parent/parents choose what subjects work best for their children's development. This means that the child might not be taught all the academic subjects they would be taught in school.

- **Traditional Home-school Method:**
This method adapts the same procedure and principles as academic/school education. Private tutors are also hired to teach the home-school student in their own home.

- **Accelerated Learning Home-school Method:**
This method has helped home-school students get into university earlier, as well as graduate from high school earlier. The accelerated home-school method is when the student can quickly move on from a subject about which they have a vast knowledge.

- **Principled Approach Home-school Method:** Purely Christian-based, this is where the home-schooled child will learn research, reasoning, recording and relating. This is all based around the word of God.

- **Online Home-school Method:**
In this final method, home-school students learn their subjects through online courses and

classes. They may be also allowed to chat with other students. However, the only problem with this type is that they are more focused on the computer teaching them, then their parents being supportive and teaching them themselves. In any type of home-school, I believe a personal bond between the parent (possible teacher) and student (possibly child of the teacher/parent) is very important for their overall mental, physical, and psychological growth.

What Type of Home-schooling did my Mum do with us?

When my mum decided to take my sister and I out of state school to home-school us, she used the following methods of home-schooling:

- **Classical Home-schooling:**

At home we were taught Maths, English, Science, some History such as the history of inventions, Essay Writing and Speed Writing. Unfortunately, because my mum could not fit every single subject into our day, we were not taught the National Curriculum History, however, this does not mean we are unable to learn it ourselves.

- **Online Home-schooling:**

My mum did not teach me every single subject under the academic educational syllabus by herself. For example, when it came to more complicated methods of maths, she found for me and my sister websites which teach a substantial number of subjects. These teach Science, Economics, Maths, Computer Sciences, Humanities and Test Preparation.

- From online home-schooling, I could learn and am still learning French and Japanese. I learned French from Rosetta Stone, while I learned Japanese from books and clips on the internet.

My sister decided she wanted to learn Spanish and has never stopped since.

- **Eclectic Home-school:**

My mum decided to choose the best subjects for us to learn. This helped us to grow and become confident and independent learners.

- **Traditional Home-school:**

My mum still taught the fundamental subjects needed for me and my sister to grow. For example, our day would consist of English Literature, English Language, Maths, Science, Art, and even for a temporary time Speed Writing. She also helped us to do independent learning, for example, watch educational videos and learn other languages by ourselves.

How did my Mother Discover Home-schooling?

There are many ways to discover home-school, for example, you can research online or talk to a friend who home-schools. The specific way my mum learned about home-schooling was from two books and a lot of research. The books she used to educate herself on home-schooling were called How to get Started in Home-school and Education Answers by John Clare.

My mum also did a lot of research into the subject, before she finally decided that home-school was the right choice, or better choice, for me and my sister.

Is Home-schooling Legal?
Home-school is legal. To be specific, it is legal in the countries of Australia, Canada, New Zealand, United Kingdom and, by 1993, home-school became legal in the 50 states of the United States of America. However, the only places that home-school has been illegal are in Germany and Sweden. Other counties will find home-schooling unacceptable; however, this does not mean it's illegal. If a parent decides to home-school their child, they need to follow a couple

of very important rules. It's also very important to research the laws relating to education and home-schooling in your country, before making any decisions.

What to do if You Decide to Home-school Your Child

If you (the parent or adult) ever decide to home-school your child, or future children, the first important thing to do is to inform the school in writing that you are going to take the child out of their care and home-school them. It's also best to copy this letter and have it sent recorded delivery, as proof that you have sent the letter to them. No matter what state or country you are in, it's important to find out and understand the laws and conditions of home-schooling in your location, since every state or country can have different rules, laws and opinions about it.

Home-school Evidence
Unfortunately, because people think home-school only consist of people who do the De-schooling/No Schooling method, the local authority should ask for evidence that you are home-schooling your child in the right way. It is still important to know these rules, especially for adults who have never home-schooled before.

Analysis Thought: Chapter 5 Explaining Home-schooling

It's important that, when someone does not know about a subject, that you are able to explain it to them correctly and in more detail. This is especially important for home-schooling, since the media likes to make home-schooling negative. This will be discussed later in Chapter 6. To find out how to explain home-schooling properly to a person, so that they understand, it would be best to go into my memory and explain my experience of home-schooling and what it is.

How did I explain Home-schooling?

Unfortunately for me, I was desperate to make any type of friends. Even in home-school I was still lonely and had nobody to be a friend in my life. Therefore, from the age of ten to twelve, I used to explain what home-school was in the wrong way. I would amaze other children about home-school by saying that you could watch television, play games, laze around and not actually study. I must admit now this was the worst way for me to represent myself and all home-schooled children.

However, I did this because my only aim was to seem "cool" enough to kids, so that they became my friends. Fortunately, my elder home-schooled sister was much more mature, and could tell other children what home-schooling was like, while scolding me for lying about the experience. After the age of fourteen, I finally realized that lying about home-school was not going to help me at all. Below are the reasons why I don't recommend you, or your children, do what I did from age ten to twelve:

• It can make you seem unintelligent and have no ambition for the future.

• It can give false impressions of your parents and how they take care of you. For example, by my saying all those negative things about home-school, it made it seem that my mum was a bad parent.

• It's not going to attract the right type of friends for you. You may only get friends who have parents who say they home-school their children, but in fact don't. You may also get bullied by these types of kids once they realize you are not the type who is lazy and does not study.

All in all, this will cause even more stress for you.

- If your parents realize that you're explaining home-school in this manner, they might question if it was right taking you out of school.

- Trying to act cool, making the wrong type of friends and lying about how home-school truly works, gives more power to the media who state that home-school is inappropriate and that it won't give children the chance to be successful or become independent in life. I know this is not true, because if I was not home-schooled and taught how to explain home-school in the right way, this book would never have been created.

How do I now go about explaining Home-schooling?

Now that I'm seventeen and learned my lessons from my family and other home-schooled people about how to explain home-school, here is how I would explain home-school to sceptics or people who don't understand.

- Home-school has the same traditional methods of academic state school learning; however, the setting is in your home and not in the classroom.

- Home-school can be for any child; however, it's mostly used for children who have disabilities (me with High Functioning Autism), children who can't cope with the state school environment, or children who have been extremely bullied.

- Home-school helps me to learn more in a quiet, peaceful, support and non-bullying environment. Because I was bullied a lot in state school, I was more focused on how to hide and who would pick on me next, instead of my homework.

- When home-schooled, our lessons are just like normal lessons; hence, we start at nine o'clock in the in the morning and finish at three o'clock in the afternoon. For me, I sometimes finished at six o'clock, and even eight o'clock, when it came to revising for IGCSE/GCSE exams.

- Home-school does not isolate you from interactions with people and other children. There are also home-school halls where children go to learn lessons or socialize with other home-school kids.

The statements above are just a few examples of how home-school can be explained to people who don't understand, or sceptics who believe the negative views of home-school.

If you explain it to them in the right way, and they still think it's a non-social/learning environment, don't feel bad, be proud that you explained what it is and didn't make up a fantasy about it.

Chapter 6: Prejudices and Myths

Even though home school for me has been a life-changing, stressful, but positive learning experience, there are still a lot of negative things about the subject. These will be in the form of prejudices and myths that people believe, read, listen to or like to make up about home-schooling.

Prejudices about Home-schooling

Throughout my life thus far, I have had the unfortunate experience of hearing people speak about home-school in a poor way. Sometimes it's not their fault they think this way, but it still hurts me when I hear some of the negative things some people say about it. For example, some negative things stated about home-school are:

- **Home-school is a Handicap:**
I find that state schools like to make it seem home-school is a handicap for children. For example, when my mum decided to take me out of school, she had to attend a meeting with all my previous state school teachers and be lectured on how she was making a terrible mistake, how home-school was bad for me, and how I would never achieve anything from being put into a home-school environment.

It was only when my mum suggested that she should observe me in the classroom of the school, that the teachers decided to say "No", thus proving that they had something to hide and that the environment I was in was not good for me at all. To be honest, I believe that state school is a handicap, since many of them never teach students how to be independent, nor have their own mindsets.

- **You don't learn anything in Home-school:**

This is only true if you are in an unschooled environment, where the parents don't teach their child anything, yet let them stay at home. With my home-school experience, I definitely learned more things that I would in my state school. For example, I learned speed writing (which somehow formed into fast typing), as well as French and Japanese. I even learnt about essay writing, how to analyse poems, and, at the age of fifteen, how to Harvard reference my work.

- **Children who are home-schooled don't study or achieve anything in their lives:**

Again this depends how the parents teach their child. As for me I achieved a lot in home-school. I learned about how to study, all the criteria for my academic subjects, how to organize my work properly, how to keep records and how to revise for exams, etc. From being taught by my mother, I also learned naturally how to be mature and how to be around adults. This has helped me to socialize more with adults than teens and sometimes even immature teens who act like kids.

- **Home-school gives the home-school child social issues, or makes them isolated:**

This false statement annoys me the most out of all the other negative statements said about home-school. Home-schooling does not make your child have social issues: it's how the parent acts towards their own children's social life that can cause social issues or isolation. For example, there are other reasons why a child in a home-school environment may seem anti-social and isolated. These reasons can be:

- The child might have a disability which hinders their social issues. If the parent does not know this, then they might take the child into home-school without addressing the core issue of why the child is antisocial.

- The child might have been bullied so much in the past that they can have trust issues, which can create social issues and isolation. This was the scenario I was in, since I thought that any child I talked to next would be a possible bully.

This meant I was very silent for a while and mostly preferred to play and learn by myself.

- The child might never have learned how to socialize with children, let alone friendly ones, in the first place. Hence, they might need to be taken to ground zero and educated, along with their necessary academic studies, about how to socialize and mix with people.

- **Home-school is expensive:**

This statement is rather interesting. Home-schooling can be expensive if you don't know how to use the resources around you to your learning advantage. For example, you can use online learning resources, buy learning resources or buy some educational books on the topics of Maths, English, Science, History, etc.

The internet is a vast place filled with almost anything you need. You can take advantage of it and learn online. On the other hand, if you believe this to be true, then there's no point in home-schooling your child. Plus, don't you think that the education and mental welfare of your child is more important than the money you may have to spend to help that child permanently?
One of my personal beliefs is that money, no matter how hard, can always be found. A child who has been scarred from state school, who has had permanent physical, mental, and

psychological damage, and has this damage affect their entire life in a negative way, is harder to heal or can't even be healed at all. It's also important to know that in home-school there will be sacrifices, hence, this means the sacrifice of time, money and even the personal life you may have outside. As a parent, who does not home-school, these sacrifices happen anyway. Why would you not sacrifice a little more to make sure the welfare of your child is positive, safe and healthy?

• You can't teach your child everything in home- school: This statement is only dependent on how much the parent who is home-schooling their child wants to teach them. My mum would fit Maths, Science, English Language, English Literature, Speed Writing, Essay Writing and French into my lessons every day.

My mum did do this by doing each subject for one hour, sometimes more if the subject was very important. It is true that I didn't learn History or Geography; however, this does not mean that home-school is bad. You can be in a mainstream state school, learning all these subjects, and still not achieve in them due to the child either not enjoying learning or being stressed from constant bullying.

Negative Reactions to Home- schooling

Now we have discussed the major myths of home- school (as well as the prejudices people have about it). I would like to discuss the tortuous situation where you can be ridiculed just for saying that you work in another environment. This does not only apply to home-school, hence, you may get negative reactions whether you like a different sport, if you have a different religion, if you a different race, or even if you are interested in boys at the age of sixteen. For me, I got the most negative reactions from saying I'm home-schooled or that I had Autism. Some negative reactions I got, when I said I was home-schooled, were as follows:

People would/might ask the following questions:

- Do you learn in home-school?
- Can you be lazy in home-school?
- Do you get out much?
- Do you have any friends?
- Your probably have no social life, right?
- How can a parent teach you home-school subjects?
- Is home-school a real school?
- Is that why you are so abnormal?

People who hear you're home-schooled might do the following actions:

- They think you are more stupid than they are and try to treat you that way.
- They may avoid you or cancel you out altogether; hence, you may experience isolation.
- They may give some offensive comments.

For example, I once heard from an immature person that my parents did the wrong thing and they might have ruined my life. Another child stated, "Ah that's why you are so weird," which was quite offensive.

- They might start giving you easy academic questions to see if you are stupid. This happened to me often, since immature kids would give me simple maths questions to test my knowledge (for example, one child asked me, "What is two plus two?") after I said I was home-schooled. This was the reason why I remained mostly on my own, since I was not ready to be ridiculed by so many other children every time I tried to socialize with them.

What I have found, over the years, is that adults are more accepting of the fact that you are home-schooled than kids. Hence, this is the reason why I am able to get along more with adults than kids and teenagers.

Analysis Thought; Chapter 6

How to Deal with the Prejudices of Home-schooling

Coping with the reactions we might get from saying we are home-schooled can be challenging, stressful, emotional and tough. However, in this analysis section, I draw up a table which shows some of the ways children and adults can deal with the prejudices about home-schooling. Thanks to my lovely mother, who helped me out in this Analysis Thought, I can get advice from her as how she dealt with people's negative reactions when they heard she was home-schooling her own two children. The table below shows some of the way my mother, my sister and I dealt with home-school prejudices:

How children can deal with it

If you find yourself receiving negative comments or reactions after telling people you are home-schooled, simply ignore them and continue. If their reactions still bother you, as they sometimes did for me, the best option would be to talk your parent or someone you truly trust about this.

Challenge their Knowledge on Home-school:

As I got older, I was feeling braver and bolder in myself. Therefore, I could sometimes challenge people on the subject by asking them if they knew what home- school was. Almost ninety-nine percent of the time the children, teenagers and some adults didn't even know where home-school originated from, or what it meant. This way, you can defend yourself, while showing that they are very judgmental and have less intelligence even than you on the subject at hand.

Improve Yourself:

You can easily show how home-school has changed you by showing the achievement and self-improvement you got from home-school. For example, an immature child might say to you, "In home-school you don't learn any languages." However, prove this wrong by seeing if you can bring a language lesson to your home-school study schedule. You might get ridiculed because the person may think you learn only simple maths, hence, prove this wrong by studying a for higher maths grade. For me, I could study IGCSE English Literature, English Language and Maths. Although I didn't pass my GCSE Maths (which I believe is due to the fact that I have Dyscalculia),

I can still revise higher level maths books and understand more mathematical questions than some teenagers in college.

How Adults can deal with It

Ignore the Adult/Person:
Whether the prejudiced person is another adult or a child, just completely ignore their remarks and reactions. People who react in this way usually rather have no true knowledge of home-school, or can be jealous that they, or their child, didn't receive it themselves. It can also be that they are jealous that your child is able to act in a mature manner, or may have more unique qualities because they are home-schooled. Whatever the true reason for their harshness, it's best just to ignore them completely.

Throw the prejudiced question or comment right back at them:

If an adult says, "Home-school is not an educationally stimulating environment," debate what type of home-school environment they are speaking about and explain the opposite. For example, you can say, "It is true that some types of home-school environment are not educationally stimulating, however, this goes the same for some types of state school. What makes you think state school is altogether a better educational environment than home-school?" If the adult you are having a debate with comes out with a reasonably satisfactory answer, agree with them but continue to debate how home-school has its own educational achievements as well. If the person you are debating with does not answer the question in a proper debating manner, or can't come up with any reasonable answer, you just prove to them that they don't know the subject. They should stop being so prejudiced and study the subject more. Whatever you do, do not get into a fight with the person you are talking to, unless they add to their prejudice something offensive about your child and how they are learning under your support and care.

Show how your child has benefited from Home-school:

What I mean by this, is to show the person who's prejudiced how your child has achieved more in home-school then in the state school they were in.

My mother did this, hence, this made her happy, as well as stopping most of the prejudiced remarks and reactions she was getting from naïve people.

I'm even able to do this with teenagers and adults, hence, once I show them my achievements, they either become less prejudiced and more positive towards me, or they go away to mind their own business.

These six solutions are the most important when dealing with home-school prejudice. There are many more solutions but everyone finds their solutions separately in their own time. There is one solution every person who thinks of home-schooling, or is home-schooling, should have. This solution is that no matter what...

Feel Proud About Home-school

Home-school was created before the institution of state school. There are many famous people and achievers who have come from a home-school background. Therefore, no matter how many negative comments and reactions you get from saying you're home-schooled or saying you are planning to home- school your child, always feel proud that you are or have made that decision. Don't feel ashamed or let others bring you down to that level. If you are giving your child the best education you can give to them, feel proud and confident in yourself. Thus, this will help your children to feel confident, since they learn most from their parent, as well as boost their views and reactions.

Chapter 7: Challenges of Home-school

As with all factors in life, there are definitely major challenges one can have when either being home-schooled, or home-schooling children as parents. In this chapter, I shall delve into the challenges my mother and I faced when it came to the subject of home-schooling.

The Challenges of Home-school: The Home-schooled Child

As a child, I enjoyed home-schooling. The learning, time slots and everything else were much easier challenges to cope with than what I received in my torture chamber of a state school. Looking back upon the challenges I faced at home-school, I would say they were stressful, however, a lot easier to find a solution to and sometimes learn to adjust to. Some of the challenges I had when I was being home-schooled were:

• New learning time schedules: Every day I woke up early, except of course at weekends. I would have lessons from nine o'clock in the morning as usual.

The challenge came when, sometimes for my assignments, I had to work until six o'clock or eight o'clock, while of course still having fifteen minute breaks every hour. For my poor mum, she had to deal with a lot from me, since I was not used to working that late and would get grumpy and easily upset. Looking back upon those times, I must admit the long working hours were worth it, since I got high grades which helped me greatly. I also thank my mum for having the patience to put up with me, since not a lot of parents would. My mum and I also got into verbal fights with each other because we were both stressed out, and naturally arguments do start in such cases. Luckily things would work out afterwards, and we would continue or finish the lesson until the next day.

• New environments: My lessons were not in my house all the time. On Wednesdays, I would go to a hall where other home-school kids went to learn lessons such as French and Maths. When I first went to the hall I was petrified, and was behind my mum's knees a lot, trying to hide from kids and their parents who would be very friendly and try to say "Hi" to me. After the experience of being hit with skipping ropes by kids, the name-calling, and having rocks thrown at me, I was not ready to suddenly open to a new set of kids.

• Having to socialize with new home-school kids: My mum always wanted the best for me, and still does. In the past, she would tell me to go and try to play or talk with the kids, instead of hanging around with her all the time. Sometimes I did try, but could not somehow form the bond that kids normally would when trying to make friends, so either I would go and sit by myself or go back to a distance close to my mum where I would still be by myself. Throughout this time at the home- schooling hall I was usually very quiet, didn't say much and focused on the homework that had to be done. This was not my mum's fault at all; it was the way I functioned as a kid.

As the years went by, the next challenge was learning the social rules, hence, what to do and not do. Unfortunately, this would lead to my getting into verbal and sometimes into physical fights with kids, because they didn't understand what Autism was and how it affects children, and I didn't understand how some actions can cause kids to get angry instead of laugh. An example of a social problem-related fight is below:

One day I was in the care of a lovely lady. She usually babysat kids and, over the road from her house, was a football ground where boys used to play football. She also had two kids of her own, which was nice for them since they had more kids to play with.

I wanted to learn to be more sociable, therefore, I was sitting on the bar near the football park watching the boys playing football. I was observing and plotting in my little brain to see how I could get in and join the game, plus make new friends along the way. It didn't matter whether the kids were boys or girls; I was desperate to make at least one friend. Suddenly I saw this boy run into the park, snatch the football up with his hands and run away with it, while the other boys were laughing, calling him an idiot, and demanding the ball back. A light bulb came on in my head and I thought, "That's it!" I thought, as soon there was an opening, I could steal the football (temporarily) and perhaps they would let me join them in their game once I gave the ball back.

Well soon enough there was an opening when the ball was kicked into the open. Even though I was an overweight kid, with all my might and gusto, I ran into the park, scooped up the ball and ran out of the park again. Because I was a girl, the reaction was very different, therefore, instead of laughing, most of them were annoyed. I realized maybe if I gave the ball back they would lighten up, therefore, as soon as two boys came over, I gently kicked the ball back to them. At that age (which was eight years old) I had a very short temper and, if angered, a very violent personality. What happened next was the straw that broke the camel's back. The boy who had the ball kicked it back in my face, called me fat, took the ball and ran off while the other boy laughed at me. I decided then and there that friends were useless and, no matter what, they were going to get a taste of their medicine.

I chased the two boys around the park, while the others inside the park were laughing and saying I was too fat to catch them. It didn't matter what those boys said; at that time, my focus was on the two boys who had offended me. Finally, I could grab one boy by his arm, made him spin in circles so he got dizzy, and threw him in the thorn bush that was close by. The way the boy fell into the thorn bush was funny to me. After that first successful attack, I broke a branch from that same bush, caught up with the boy who kicked the ball in my face, and violently started to whack him everywhere with the thorn bush. I was whacking his head, arms and legs, but mostly the head because he was begging for me to stop and crying for help, therefore this meant he felt the most pain there. I wanted to show them how painful it felt to be alone, having to deal with isolation and bullying over the years and how their action was wrong.

Luckily my mother and the babysitter came out a few seconds later, ran over the road and separated the fight. I was kicking, crying and screaming insults for three minutes before my mum calmed me down enough to have me explain to the story to her. "I see what you were trying to do, but it was not the best way to socialize," my mum calmly told me. I was confused about why the boy could do this but when I did the same thing, I got a negative result. After that, I decided to become isolated and quiet so I would not be hurt in that way again by such children.

Looking back upon that memory, I realised it was the wrong thing to do, however, social rules are not as easy as pie. Sometimes when you are an alien in a neuro-typical world, you are following instructions or actions to get something positive at least from others.

An important tip I'll give to parents is this; if your child seems to be getting into fights and is alone, don't assume it's entirely their fault, or that they are just bad naughty kids. There are too many people in this world ready to batter, belittle and judge your children without understanding them. Don't become those people; since your child loves and needs your understanding, support and love the most. Try to find the reason why this is happening, what could be fuelling their anger and, if you have not done so already, get them diagnosed. A diagnosis to check if your child may have a disability could make things easier to understand if they do have one, since you can research it, find its effects and the solutions for those kids with anti-social problems.

• Coping with more homework: Along with the long working hours were also more subjects to learn. In my typical home-school day, I would need to fit in all lessons about Maths, English Literature, English Language, French, Essay Writing, Comprehension and Science. For me, sometimes all these lessons would be overwhelming (due to information overload). At the beginning of home-school, I would have headaches from all the learning, or try to avoid lessons at home altogether by sleeping late or past the time that mum would start lessons. Fortunately, my mum was very strict and always got me to work on my lessons even if it was two hours later.

The homework I had the most difficulty with was Comprehension. I knew this was due to my Receptive and Expressive Disorder, hence, when I thought I answered a question correctly, I had somehow not answered it right. This, of course, made me bitter and angry and, in the end, crying because learning to understand and answer correctly was so difficult for me.

The Home-school Parent/Teacher

As well as the home-school child having challenges of their own, I feel in my opinion it's more challenging for the home-schooling teacher/parent because they must deal with negativity from others and the peer pressure to be in an unrealistically normal world. For me, it is like: if you are not with the others, like a group of sheep, you then get slated by the other mindless people who are really wolves in sheeps' clothing. The challenges my mother went through when home-schooling me were:

• Setting a new school routine: I admit I was not always the perfect child. When I was home-schooled, I enjoyed being at home so much that at times I would aim to avoid the work I needed to do like the plague. Luckily my mother was strict and always somehow straightened me out and got me back to my homework. Even today when I am too stressed with homework, my mind will go tight and buzz. Therefore, this would make me moody, tired, ill and I would leave my homework until the next day. When I was home-schooled, it was vital for me to pass my grades for college, so I would be doing all my academic work.

Important note: As you can guess, for me ten hours of work (one hour of work followed by fifteen minute breaks) was way too much for my young mind to take in as a new routine. Although it's known that some Autistic children love routine, I was one of those Autistic children who hated routine and became very bored and irritated by it. This frustration came out most in tantrums, fits, anger and crying fits. Luckily my mum persisted with me to achieve, even when she was tired of me, she never gave up on me. I shall stress that the one thing any child needs, whether Autistic, disabled or not, is patience.

For an Autistic child who thought themselves worthless because their school treated them like this, and got angry any time I made a natural mistake (due to the teachers being mad at me when I made a small mistake) my mother had to learn to reset my thinking about making mistakes and be patient with me when my small incorrect answers made me cry, frustrated or storm from the room in rage. Till this day, I still love and thank my mum for that.

- **Pressure from others:**

Unfortunately my mother went through the negative pressure, opinions and negative prejudices about home-schooling. When I asked my mum if anyone ever told her she was wrong for taking me out of school, my mum nodded and said, "Yeah, there were loads of examples, however, I didn't care about their Opinions. I knew home-schooling was the best for you, rather leaving you in that state school never to learn and use your full potential." She explained further how people would ask her why she took me out of school; would she be able to deal with a child who had Autism; how she would be stunting my social growth, and of how state school would have been a much better place for me to stay in. My mother and I definitely know that, if I stayed in school, I would have been so different. I would not be the kind, humble, ambitious and strong person today; also, I know I definitely would not be writing this book. I know I would have been one of the negative statistics: those people with a disability whom society believed never would have succeeded in anything, as my teachers told my mother in school to "give up on her".

Analysis Thought: Chapter 7

How your struggles and challenges will pay off (for the home-schooling teacher/parent)

As I said before, I have a high respect for all parents, because it takes a lot to raise a new life from a defenceless new-born to the best child they can be. At times, you, the parent, may have felt like giving up, thinking it's hopeless, or that you're not a good parent. For the home-schooling parent, it's ten times harder; because you're the parent as well as the teacher of your child, and how you educate them will have a massive impact and effect in the future. There were times where my mum almost gave up and almost had a breakdown, since she was a single mum with two kids, having to be the role of mother, father and teacher to the both of us. No one (especially my mum) ever deserves to have to do three difficult positions at time, but sometime life is cruel and unfair.

No matter how hard things get, I stress deeply never to give up on your child. Never hinder them or give up on them because, once you know you have done your best, they will do all they can to pay you back for the stress and pain you went through in the past for them. What's more important is that the love of your child should be stronger than the pain you are going to go through with them as they grow up and learn about the world. For all those parents (including home-schooling parents), from my experience, I'll give the reasons and results you get from being strong and never giving up on you child. Some positive results you get for being strong and sticking it through are:

- **Your child becomes more independent:**

For me, I could face a lot more challenges and do a lot more things for myself, because my mum put in the effort to teach me how important it was to be self-efficient and independent. This is how I could write eBooks, sell eBooks, do self-study for college assignments and exams, and overall become a confident person. It's important to teach your child independence, not only in the home, but also when it comes to outside factors, and pressure they could face outside. It gives them strong grounds to build upon, and it also boosts their confidence immensely.

- **Your child will love and respect you more:**

I know home-schooling a child must be difficult, hard and stressful. This is what makes me love my mum and respect her more, because she sacrificed a lot for me without wanting anything in return.

- **Your child will go through hell to succeed in life just to make you proud:**

I'm always doing everything I can to make sure my mum's arduous work and dedication didn't go to waste. For example, I write eBooks, get paid and then give her a share of the profits I make. I also do other things for my mum to make sure she's proud of me.

- **How to Deal with a Stressed Home-school Child**

To help parents, who are home-schooling their children to deal with a stressed home-schooled child, I decided to go to my mother to ask for her advice, as well as what she did to deal with me when I got stressed over homework and studying. Mum answered with her usual words of wisdom, hence, I have taken her answers and converted them into advice for you to use when you are dealing with your child in stressful home-schooling times. The tips I discovered were:

- **Patience:**

When I was at state school and got a question wrong, I was always scolded and made to feel stupid by the teachers. I was taught never to make mistakes, for if I did, it would be detrimental. This is the worst lesson ever to learn and should not be taught, since it's natural and good to make mistakes so you learn from them. My mum said she was learning from me; hence, what she was learning was to be patient with me. When I was studying at home and got a question wrong, I would get very stressed and worked up; even in the end crying, kicking objects, throwing items at walls and refusing to do my other studies.

Although sometimes my mum told me off for acting in such a way, she also understood that I was taught the wrong life lessons in school. This meant she must be the one to correct my thinking pattern, and that required a lot of patience. I am very thankful to my mum today for taking the time and stress to deal with me, even in the hardest of times. My mum taught me through her patience to be humble and kind to others. This means I rarely ever get mad unless the cause is heart-breaking or wrong for me.

- **Focus your child on another topic:**

If one topic is making your home-schooled child angry, frustrated or upset, and it's getting too much for you to handle, focus your child on another topic and try the difficult topic later. When I was stressed over a topic (for example comprehension, because it challenged my receptive skills and I got almost every question wrong), my mum would then give me a break of about fifteen minutes before I went to focus on another academic subject.

I remember sometimes going off to cool down,

play with toys, or even draw, just so I could calm down and focus the next topic.

It's very important that you focus the child on another topic (after taking a short break from studying) rather than forcing them to tackle it. Forcing them to do that task on the same day will only stress out the child more and cause more stress for you. It's best if you get the child to complete as many topics as possible, without an extreme amount of stress, then focus them on the difficult topic the next day.

- **Talk to your child about their Issues and difficulties:**

As a child with Autism, no matter how much my mum pushed me to make friends, it somehow didn't work for me. This made me depressed and miserable, because as I worked in my home on my subjects, I would hear other kids playing outside. For me it was heart-breaking to have to see and listen to a part of social life I didn't have a clue how to create. I remember asking my mum, "What is wrong with me?" and "Why can't I go out and play?" My mum sat with me and would explain to me the reasons, which were valid, and afterwards I finally understood. It's important at all time to answer your children's questions, especially when it comes to home-schooling and any that are related to a disability that may be affecting their life.

Failure to do this can damage a child's mind and make them feel alien or that it's entirely their fault. It can even make them think they are stupid and worthless. It is always important to reassure your child when they feel discouraged or lost in life.

- **Treat your child by taking them out to places:**

Home-schooling is not all about work, and should never just be about work. For a young child, getting out and learning is key, especially when they are having fun. When I was home-schooled, I used to go through a lot of pain from being lonely. My mother realized I was not going out as much and decided she would change that. She was learning along with me how to be the best home-schooling parent. She resolved this loneliness by taken me out to place, for example, the Science Museum, Natural History Museum, and other places of fun and learning such as social groups. When I was not studying, my mother would take me to the cinema, the toy store or even the park.

This helped me to forget my issues and worries Autism was having for me and made me enjoy life a lot more. It's important to treat your child to going out somewhere, especially if they are putting in the effort into their work (whether home-school or state school). It gives them the lesson that smart/demanding work pays off, and this will help them in future with college, university and beyond.

I hope these tips have helped you adults who home-school your children. These are the solutions my mum used for me and, although each child is different, I hope one of these solutions gives a powerful and positive result, just as they did for me.

How to deal with home-school and Autism blues (for the home-school child or teen)

This section is especially dedicated to children and teenagers who have Autism or/and are or have been in home-school, and are feeling terribly lonely. Even for me today, I still dread holidays and breaks because most of the time I'm at home sitting around doing nothing. Although I still go through these times, there are things I do for myself which not only cheer me up, but keep me distracted till the time when I won't be by myself so often. The things I usually do when I feel down and lonely are:

- **Go through the emotions:**

The worst thing to do is to completely ignore your emotions and pretend nothing is wrong. It's just the same as bottling up your feelings inside, which can cause illness and even more pain within. When you feel down, depressed and even want to cry, just let it out and go through the motions. Accept that you're a sensitive person and that it's ok to feel down at certain points in life.

- **Write in a diary or journal:**
I am terrible at keeping diaries and journals, since I don't feel the need to write in one often. But for other people, writing down your pain and feelings is the best way to get rid of pain and stress.

- **Push yourself out of the comfort zone:**
Although I am lonely, one of the hardest things for me to do is to go out to places, even if it's just by myelf to get fresh air. If you're a person who stays inside a lot (due to having no friends to go out with), and feels nervous to go out on your own, what I advise is to start pushing yourself out of the comfort zone, but at your own pace.

An example I can give is a time when I was feeling the same way; however, I decided to push myself by just going to a park and staying there for an hour. I was really and truly scared, however, after I did it, I felt proud of myself and more confident to go to places, and even till today, I'm still practising pushing myself out of my comfort zone.

- **Try talking to people casually online:**
It's important to stress that when you're talking to anyone online, never arrange to meet them on your own. If you ever decide to meet someone who you've met online, take a family member or several close friends with you. For me, I was inside a lot, hence, this cut down my communication a lot and, due to my Autism, it made it a lot harder for me to meet and talk to others. It's affected me deeply, since the constant silence in my home made me silent and almost never want to talk. Using online social networks to talk to others was a training session for me, hence, my communication improved by first talking to people online.

It's important to stress as well not to depend just on online sources to communicate. Only use that as the first stage, then as you get better, push yourself out of the comfort zone and start going to social events.

Feeling pain and struggles.

The biggest pain and struggles for me were the social understanding and communication around me. Even though my mum did her best to take me to places with kids, and places of importance such as museums, arcades, and sent me to camps with other kids, my social understanding and communication were so different, that instead I would end up having disagreements with kids, being isolated or have fights happening. Looking back at those times where fights started, I knew some of them were not my fault, however, I also understand that I should have responded in a mature way; rather than I was I did at the age of eight.

Below are different examples of when I had communication issues:

- **The church camp incident:**

A boy at the church camp I was at stole my sister's dairy. My sister demanded it back but the boy called her fat. My sister seemed pretty ticked off but calm about the situation, however, for me at that age, I didn't know how to respond with a witty remark or anything else for that matter. My body was hot and my fists were clenched, therefore, I understood at that time they only way for me to respond was to attack the boy who was mean to my elder sister. As soon as the boy's guard was off (he was laughing with his eyes closed), I lunged at him, and started to choke him while he had a sweet in his mouth. I know to this day I could have killed him, however, at that time I was not thinking that way, and my anger told me it was better to punish him for how nasty he was. I received a sharp blow to my arm by the boy, but didn't care at all; all I knew at that time was that he deserved it.

The boy and I had to apologize to each other afterwards, however, I didn't mean the apology one bit at that time.

- **The shoe incident:**

As we all know boys will be boys, however, at the worst of times, boys at an early age (who have not yet learned manners) can be disrespectful and disgusting. I found this out at my home-schooling classroom where this boy kept on teasing me constantly, calling me rude names and being sarcastic, which I never understood due to the fact that my Autism didn't help me to comprehend it as fast as my sister did. One day I finally had enough and decided to face this boy once and for all, hence, I walked up to him and told him to stop bullying me, calling me names and how immature and silly it was to bully another person. The result I got was not positive, since instead of apologizing, he had the bravery to spit on my new clean 'flower-girl' shoes which I was wearing. I was enraged, since the shoes were open-toe and my mum had recently brought the shoes for me. Therefore, the result of this disgusting action was that I chased him around the home-school building, while at the same time shouting and being in tears. I could punch him once on the arm, but after that, his dad stopped him and gave him a firm scolding.

The boy was made by his father to apologise to me afterwards and that was the end of that. My mum was happy that I decided to not attack the boy straight away, which was what I normally did when I was angry at eight years old, but she did tell me not to throw the first punch. In my opinion, spitting at anyone, whether it's on them, a family member or their belongings, is equivalent to punching them.

Seeing your Child Isolated.

Isolation is one of the most painful feelings ever to experience or witness, especially if you see your own child in this way whether they're home-schooled or in state school. My mum knew my struggles to socialize were strong, and she would have to help me though the tears and pain to get better. "It's not you who's the problem," she would tell me, "Things will get better. Trust me". Although my mother was right, the situation of sitting alone all the time, while other kids were playing, was still a huge burden to deal with.

For any child, bullying can be the worst thing, especially when you're in places where you are meant to enjoy your childhood and have fun. An example of this was when I was going to Wales with one of the other families who were home-schooled. They were a great friendly family and decided to take me with them since they knew of my issues and Autism. I thought it was going to be great and I would have the best time ever. However, this family also decided to bring another family along with them to Wales, whose children were not the friendliest.

During that week in Wales, there was a total of five children huddled in a rented old cottage in the small village. In the case of five children, if one child could make the other four laugh at his jokes or get along with him, then bullying became easy. Unfortunately, since I was timid, trying to control my flaring temper and be good for my mum's sake, this little punk made fun out of me for every small thing I did. This included how I talked, explained things (which didn't come out right) and many more things. In the end, I spent the rest of the week walking around the back stables and garden of the house trying to hide from everyone and deal with the pain alone.

At that time, I didn't want anyone to know that I was upset, hence, I used to pretend everything was ok as if nothing was happening. I never recommend anyone to do this, since it makes you weak, sick, and in the worst cases can even kill you. When I returned home I remember my mum looking at me with her beaming face and big smile asking how the trip went. I was doing all I can to say it went well and I had a wonderful time, but instead I burst into tears and told her about the bullying and everything else I went through. At that time, I felt ashamed because mum was doing so much for me and the fact that I was not having fun made me feel like I was ungrateful or failing her. After that trip, I never attended another one with that family again.

Having a Single Mother.

I take my hat off to all single mothers of the world who may be in a struggle but are yet pushing through and making sure they give the best to their kids. My beloved mother was a single mother to me and my sister, and before that, to our elder brother. She was always strong and never showed how much the divorce affected her. However, during the home-school time and the stress of taking care of me, my father didn't help the situation with his actions and antics.

An example was when our dad decided to give us his girlfriend's old clothes, instead of new fresh casual clothes from the shops. My dad was not a poor man, hence, I understand now why, when I showed the clothes to mum, her face was drained of all calmness and happiness. At that time I was afraid, because I didn't understand how heartless it was to do that, and I thought I had done something wrong. Mother did reassure me that I did nothing wrong but her voice was stiff and filled with compressed anger.

It was also not helpful when my dad made comments about how being in state school was so much better. These were followed by the fact that my mother had to deal with problems from his side, such as his mother telling me I needed to lose weight. As if I didn't have enough bullying issues already to deal with as a kid. My mother had to become the mum and dad all in one, being strict with us when we were naughty, while taking care of finance, the house, my disability, my sister, bullying and everything else that comes with a single mother's life. Without mum, I would not be the self-respecting strong person I am today.

Trusting someone else with your child.

While I was home-schooled, terrible news struck that my grandmother, from my mother's side, passed away from old age. It was a blow to my mum's spirits, and although she stayed strong through that time, she also had to deal with a divorce. Since mum had to deal with funeral arrangements, she had no choice but to bring in a babysitter to take care of me and my sister while she was away. Dad might have been another option, but he was gone, always said he was working and seemed too busy even to take care of us for a weekend.

My mum got in contact with an agency and a babysitter was arranged to come and take care of me and my sister. Unfortunately, this is where things in my childhood turned from bad to worse. The babysitter, who was meant to take care of me, instead abused me. She would tell me off and hit me, sometimes even for no reason at all. This went on for a while, until my mum could see something was wrong. I was quiet, tense, very scared of the baby sitter and cried constantly. My elder sister finally told my mum what was going on, and since my mum had cameras around the house already, she finally got a clip of the baby sitter hitting me and locking me in my room while I was screaming and crying to come out.

My mum did the right thing, therefore she fired the babysitter and called the police. However, because the police were at that time too slow to act, the baby sitter could move quickly and escape any charges or court case. My mum is a strong fighting woman and didn't leave it there. Instead she made sure the story went into the newspapers and even on a morning TV show. I remember being in the room behind the stage where the show was filmed. I remember afterwards watching mum from behind the scenes, as she sat in smart clothing on the chair, explaining her story and saying how mothers should not trust every single babysitting agency that says they do checks on people.

We were never able to catch that babysitter, but the newspaper and show were strong enough to send a message and warning.

Favouritism.

This topic does not just relate to parents; it can be with anyone else whom your child looks to try do their best for, but then becomes discouraged because that person is showing favouritism to somebody else. Since people with Autism can be more emotional and sensitive and things affect them ten times more, it can be stressful and upsetting when somebody is showing that someone else is better than they are, due to natural talents.

My first experience of favouritism was at the age of fourteen, where my art teacher constantly complimented another student's natural great ability at art, while always saying there was something wrong with my art, and at times paying less attention to me when I needed it. The reason it was extremely painful for me was, because I didn't only have this with the teachers at state school beforehand, but also with my father who at that time saw his girlfriends as more important than me and my sister. My mum could see the effect it was having, since I felt useless and didn't bother to talk any more to anybody. Fortunately, my mother and even my private maths tutor were there to tell me the most important advice ever. The important advice was, "Never think someone else is better than you". They also explained that it's natural for other people to be better at some topics than you, however, it does not mean you are useless, unworthy or that they are better all round than you. Since I heard that advice, I've always been strong and dealt with the constant irritation where someone else shows favouritism over me.

Child's Possible Suicidal Issues:

Again throughout this situation, I don't ever remember my father ever coming to assist. This made me damaged, feel hate, scared of all adults and have impulses to hurt or even kill something. It didn't help my suicidal issues resulting from previous bullying and neglect from my father and his side of the family. It's important to stress that if your child ever says that he/she feels like life is not worth living, they would rather be dead or tries anything to end their life, don't leave them without any help. That's the worst thing you can do. This is also for people, if they see someone close to them saying the same thing, trying the same thing, or even putting such a message on places like Facebook. No matter where you find it, don't ignore it; help them. The box below explains, from my previous experience, what it's like when you feel like ending your life. It's important to know since you can understand a person's mindset and help them.

My View of What's it like when you feel Suicidal

Anyone who has been through the experience of despair, loneliness and depression, knows the feelings of pain when, finally, they feel like the only way to save them is to end their own lives. From my point of view and experience, everything seemed gloomy and dark.

My first sign of feeling suicidal was when I was six years old and I wanted to drink a cup of bleach from the bathroom. At that point I felt lost and confused, and, since my mother told me about God, I thought the only solution that was left was to return to him before my time. Luckily, I avoided that option.

The next experience of feeling suicidal was when I was seventeen years old. This was due to having no friends at college, feeling bad because I didn't have a boyfriend (while others did and showed off) and a few other traumatic events. The first sign of my thoughts to end my life came when I woke up in the morning and I wished I was not alive. Each day for me was a struggle, and as I walked down the street, I would consider the road and wonder if I should walk into it and end it all.

When you feel suicidal, you feel empty and dark inside, because it feels like no-one can see you, hear you, or even want to be around you. For me, I spent many nights crying myself to sleep and feeling empty. I even slept throughout the entire day because I felt dreaming was a happier way to live than facing real life. Feeling suicidal was like drowning in water as the feeling to end your life would fill and suffocate you so much. For me, I was in the drowning stage, splashing and kicking in a sea of lost hope, hate, self-loathing, sadness, depression and negative memories. Something was telling me to give in and drown, while my kicking and splashing was a voice telling me to fight it and live.

Only recently at the age of eighteen have I surfaced from this destructive mind set, and have found the will to live. One of the motivations to write this book was to help others, and to warn others never to ignore someone who is feeling this way and in a worse state of mind than I could ever be.

Chapter 8: My Exam Years

For any child, whether they are home-schooled or not, their final academic exams will happen before heading to the world of college and teenage-hood. For me it was very scary, since I was home-schooled and my learning span (how much I could learn at once) was just a two-hour period. After two hours, I would become very distracted and not focus on my work. Fortunately, my mum had a few solutions to help me though my work and grades, focus on study and overall create a more independent studying mind.

How my mum helped me though my studying
There are a lot of factors that can be changed or to take note of when a child (whether home-schooled, disabled or not), is studying. From my experience, the following show what a child like me needed and had used to help me focus and prepare for exams. The factors are:

Learning Environment

- **Home Tutors:**

If you plan to home-school your child, or are doing this, it's almost a guarantee that you're going to need the help of home tutors. Some parents can take being the teacher and parent themselves. However, some parents may find it stressful to take on two very life-changing and growth-growing positions with their child. Therefore, they will need to hire a home tutor.

I advise for all parents that when they are looking for home tutors, don't just pick anyone who offers to teach your child. From my experience of Autism, it was key that mum chose a tutor who didn't misunderstand me, didn't get impatient and taught me in the right way. Fortunately, with mum's keen eye, cautiousness and care, most of the tutors mum chose for me were understanding, taught me the right way and helped me get the grades.

There was also one terrible experience too which I will never forget.

Why you should listen when your child says they are not learning

As a child, I could still sense if someone was using my mum or anybody to get something. It was a small gut feeling that tingled in my stomach, liver and back. Therefore, it gave me the message that person was trying to do something unpleasant. When I was home-schooled, I had a private science teacher. He would teach, but not in the correct format, nor to help students progress in their work.

He would mock some of the other students who were more disabled than me, therefore, making more worry and stress for them. He would not pay deep attention to me whether I was learning or not. He would just tell me to read the science books mum got for me, memorize and take notes. This was not my learning style, and I didn't know how to take down notes properly either. I would literally copy everything from the book on to paper, just because I thought that was the way to take notes. After a while I realized I was not learning at all, and I became very depressed as it came closer to my exams. He would mock me as well; however, because I didn't understand I was being mocked, he was able to get away with most of it.

When I heard my mum was bringing the same teacher over to do private lessons at my house (as well as pay him for his useless tutoring), I told mum not to do it. I explained everything and that the fact that I was not learning. "Just do your best, and although you're right, he is the only science tutor we have got," my mum would reply. After saying the same thing a few more times I gave up. I guessed mum knew what she was doing. I understand how why she kept the teacher, even though he used mum and was not very good. She would have preferred for me to receive any education, rather than none. That's the true power of a mother's love.

I felt disgusted every time the science tutor came to the house, taught me plainly without any explanation about my lesson, told me to memorize cards and what was in the book, before being paid five pounds to head home. In the end, I got an F in science, which didn't help my confidence, and made mum realize she really should not have paid that tutor to teach me.

There is a positive end to that experience, since when I went to college I got straight distinctions in my Applied Sciences (with only two assignments at merit grade). However, that is for another book. It's also important to know that when a parent home-schools their child, they can make mistakes as well. It's all part of the learning process for both parent and child.

It's also very important that the home tutor you hire gets along with your child. It's true; we must deal with people we may not like in life. However, for a child, anyone that's with the child during the education years up to college will have a massive impact on their growth, self-worth, education and what they think about themselves and their future. If a child is given to anyone, without supervision or checks, it can cause negative consequences and for the child's life and their views to be affected negatively.

The tutor I got on most with was my maths teacher. He was a cheerful old man who understood me, was patient when I didn't 'get' maths, and didn't belittle me when I got a D in maths. Although he was strict at times, he understood my learning difficulties, frustration and pain, and helped me get out of those times. I'm thankful for that maths teacher for giving me strength, not only in maths, but also my view on life itself and how to get though the tough times. The most important lesson my maths tutor taught me was, "Never think anyone else is better than you." Hence, it's helped me build my confidence and, in another book, explain the story about how I faced other people who tried to belittle me in educational and life environments.

Work Organization

- **How work is stored**

In the field of studying and revision, one of the key elements is the recording and storing of work and important documents you need to succeed. In this section I think it will especially help parents and children by telling my story of how I organized and stored my work. Some of the ways I was taught to do this by my mother were:

- **Folders:**

As soon as I went into home-school, I was taught how to record and file my homework. When I go to colleges these days, I see how so many students have trouble finding their homework, how their papers are just stuffed into folders, how some of their homework is even on the floor of classrooms and how some just stuff study notes into their bags instead. It's not unusual to get admiration, stares and the comment, "Wow you're so organized!" when I come in to class with a huge bag containing my folder. It's very important to teach your kids, home-schooled or not, about why, when and how it's important to file homework and other important documents. They are going to need it in future; hence, why not start now and get the difficult learning process done sooner?

- **Record sheets:**

My mum is a very organized person. She has had to be this way so she can record her documents. When I was revising for my IGCSE/GCSE topics, my mum introduced me to the sheets she used to keep track of records and find them quickly when needed. I was confused and annoyed, since I was never taught in school how to file homework properly before. However, after a few trials and errors, I saw how important they were and how easier life got when filing work in them.

- **USB keys:**

When it came to USB keys, my mother taught me so much about organization, that learning how to organize work on an USB key was a lot easier, as well as knowing I could easily do it myself. The method I used was to make folders on the course topic, then which unit, which assignment (or notes), then file the information and work about that topic in that folder.

One thing I would definitely recommend for a child in any type of education is to take on a beginner Microsoft course or a course relating to IT or computer basics. They usually teach students about each Microsoft program on the computer, how they work and how it will be helpful to them in future.

- **Study diary:**

Another key point is to keep a study diary. This diary is especially made to record what academic subjects you have learned that day, how many are left to be learned, and if not all of them are learned, write what needs to be done tomorrow. As a home-schooled child, this helped me immensely, since my memory was not the best. Writing things down in a diary helped me to look back and remember what needed to be done.

- **Exams: How I prepared for them**

As the exams were coming closer and closer, I admit I had terrible anxiety (which I didn't know at the time) and a lot of fears. My mum encouraged me by telling me that, if you prepare yourself beforehand and do the best you can in anything, you will face your result with no guilt or regret.

My mother also taught me if I didn't succeed to try again and not give up until you achieve the exact goal you want. Taking on my mother's wise words, I decided I would do my best, as well as use my own strategies to be prepared for all my exams. The ways I prepared for my exams (which may help children as well as parents) are:

- **Independent learning:**

As much as a parent is there to support their child, be with them and help them with their studies, there is a certain point where the parent is unable to be with their child all the time during study periods. Therefore, it's very important to teach independence to a child at an early age, instead of when they are going through their most stressful period in the transition to teenage life (exams) where the teenager requires more responsibility and a lot more independence.

What my mum used to do was tell me to go to revise a subject while she was busy with other tasks in the house. It didn't matter whether I fully understood or not; if I attempted to study on my own, that was the key point. On the subjects I did know, mum would leave me to revise them by myself and would only help if I really needed it. This is where the study diary came in handy, since it told me what subjects I did yesterday and what subjects I needed to study next, to balance and learn all the subjects I needed to know.

- **Note cards:**

When I got a question wrong, needed to remember a science subject or needed to know what a simile was, my mum encouraged me to make small note cards and, before bed, reread though them. I admit I was not comfortable with going through the notes every day, but looking back I see what this method of learning was so important to my learning process and memory. It helped increase my memory and remind myself about topics which I didn't know.

My Personal View on the Education Process these Days

I decided to write my own personal view on education, because, in today's world, I feel we are not being taught to create with our minds, but to remember from the past. I'm not saying the past is not important; however, I feel we are focusing too much on remembering, instead of discovering and finding new things to empower our world. For example, in English literature and language, we are taught only to write a review or answer to a question from a specific book. Another example is that we all must learn every single maths equation beforehand, instead of learning new and easier ways to find the same answers to the same questions. I'm not saying that we must not learn these subjects, but I feel we humans of this world are just living on recycled information.

Even fashion decides to go back in time to find modesty and class instead of finding the unique style of fashion none has ever found before. What also disturbs me is how exams judge us, and sometimes even how we view ourselves and how we should live, on a few exam paper methods, points and results. The ways results are given and received is like this: if you get a low grade you are not going to succeed. You might as well not look or jump high, which is not true because many have succeeded in a way that does not follow the pack. You can't have an all-round result on whether a person is good or not just on the letter of a grade nor on how many points they got.

I feel our system is working in this way because the only thing we are meant to be is workers, not entrepreneurs, people who think on their own or who are creative people. Yet there are so many people in the world who wonder why our generation's minds are bored, or why they have nothing better to do than to cause trouble. If a system is putting self-limiting beliefs on them, they will follow it and only give back the same thought-pattern results. How can our system focus on success and growth if we only focus on the past, and not change an education system that is just there for money and slave-making, instead of finding each person's God-given talent and using it for the better?

Results

- **How I felt:**

As I waited for my results, a lot of fears went through my mind, I prayed I passed, I hoped I did nothing wrong, I hoped mum would be still proud of me and love me after she saw the results, and many other things. In a nutshell, my results were that I passed my IGCSE English Literature and Language, got a B in my Art GCSE, but had the failing grades of F in Science, E in Maths and E in French. As a child trying to prove to the world my mum's challenging work was not a waste of time, I felt horrified about my fail results.

I cried for days, and thought I had failed mum. I even thought about how I should not be living, or how I should return to state school because I felt I failed my family so much.

Fortunately, as some parents do, they may not be happy overall, but if you tried really hard, they will still comfort you and tell you how much they love you. Mum told me she still loved me,;I was not stupid as I thought at that time and that we could always revise. It has now taken me three more maths exams and revision before getting my C in Maths. I have understood that something may be delayed for me to get, just because I need more understanding and learning, hence, at the age of nineteen going on twenty years old, I finally got my C in maths. C may not be as great as an A; but I feel proud because I put in a lot of night revision, sweat, pain and tears to get that mark. Your success is not determined by your grades; it's by how much persistence and effort you put into that goal to achieve it.

Analysis Thought: Chapter 8

- **How to help you and your child deal with exam results**

As I'm sure every adult knows, once the exams are done, the waiting period has to be completed, and we finally get our results around August. The results can either give an overwhelming sense of joy, or an insidious downward spiral leading to a false perception which appears real, called doom. In this Analysis Chapter, I explain the best way (from my experience) to help your child deal with exams and what the best things are to do and not do. This is for children who have taken the time to study and put all their effort in, and you know they have been revising and working smart instead of doing nothing. Below are the Do's and Don'ts.

Do's

- Congratulate your child. If they are upset, let them be upset but afterwards teach them that, in life, one needs to try again a few times before reaching their dream.

- Still treat your child to a day out, an event, or something they like to show you are still proud of them.

- Offer them self-help books on study, revision and confidence. My mum gave me books about these topics after my exams and reading them helped me become more confident for my retakes.

- Assist them in their retake studies. Sometimes after exams a child needs their parent to go through the work for their retakes. It's also a natural bonding process which every parent and child needs together. It gives the child the knowledge that you as the parent are supporting them.

Dont's

- Tell your child how unhappy and disappointed you are in them. This is only right if you know they have put no effort into getting their grades. But remember that if they get low grades for this reason, you must reflect on yourself and see if you did all you could, or could have done better.

- Don't punish them unless they put no effort whatsoever into their work. If they did make an effort, and they still didn't get the highest grade, don't give them a punishment. This can make a child more upset, fearful to retake any future exams and make them feel worthless.

- Don't compare your child's grades and intelligence to another child's. Not only is that cruel, but also it really won't give your child the confidence or willpower to achieve. You will just be showing that you may want to turn your child into someone they are not, or that you want that other child rather than them.

The main message is: unless it's the right type of discipline, if your child ever feels they are worthless, that they should not have been born, that you seem to find another child better than them, or the child wishes they were someone else because you would like them to be; then you have failed them and yourself as a parent. Period. Your role is to help, nurture and encourage, not compare, belittle and bring down.

- Tell other parents how your child did. If you're going to do this, make sure you child is out of earshot. If you do this while they hear you, it can bring them embarrassment, shame and guilt. Remember also that if other children hear about it, bullying can easily start, and that would be your fault, as well as your responsibility to solve.

Next Steps after Exams

The next steps were college. Unfortunately to go through that whole story here would be too much; but as I stood at the entrance to my college (at the age of 16), I was more confident and prepared, but still scared, and ready for any living monster in the form of a human to challenge me. As dramatic as it sounds, it's important to know that there are just as many challenges for a home-school child in state college, as there were in a state school and home-school beforehand. The tale of my teenage-hood will be explained in my next book.

Chapter 9: Ready for Home-school?

This is where my childhood story ends, concludes, and evaporates into the matter of space, and into the atoms of my mind's memories. Through this journey called 'life' thus far, I have learned so many things - I believe - even more than the average child. Although my Autism and other disabilities seem like a setback; at the same time, they have been one of the greatest gifts God could bless me with. I have reviewed my life so far and understood how home-school has helped me so much. I hope the advice and review I give in this concluding chapter helps you to understand what home-school can give you (if you're the child) and the benefits of doing it for your child (if you're the parent who's thinking about doing this). The ways home- school have improved me are:

• Confidence: State schools were always aiming to crush me down.

• Independent learning: Without home-school I would have not learned how to be independent in learning academic subjects, but also in my social and personal life. I feel now I can do anything and achieve anything, because my mum, tutors and my own higher self has enlightened me.

- Independent thinking: whether in schools, colleges, or in a life filled with media expectations, independent thinking can be one of the hardest things to keep or attain when you're in an environment that pressurizes you to fit into a certain group or criteria. An Autistic child could have a tough time trying to fit in, if his or her mindset is not of that of others and we do all know how cruel some kids can be. Therefore, it brings stress and hinders his or her spirit if the person is constantly made fun of, rejected and left alone in that environment.

At least, if nothing else for me, home-school has helped me to have independent thinking. I know I don't have to have the latest brand of clothes or be a size eight, just to be regarded as normal. At school my circumstances were very different; I thought if I could not get out of this, I would become a bully myself just to survive. It's shameful to admit, since I said bullying is wrong, but back then I had no one to turn to, not even the teachers who were meant to protect me from this bullying in my school. It was either fight them or join them and I was on the brink of joining them, because I could not stand another miserable day sitting alone on the playground bench, watching others play while I forced my tears back trying to be stoical. No child should ever go through what I went through and that's why home-school is one of the best things for children like me, or for any child, because it gives them independent thinking from an early age.

•   To face my enemies: Most children will face bullies, and that's a natural part of life. But for me, I had to face more enemies than the usual child. The examples were abusive babysitters and an unloving father, as well as his side of the family being belittling. This does not make me any better than any other person; however, these types of struggles are not faced by every child in life and I feel proud that I faced them head-on.

•   Never to make what someone tells you become reality: The teachers in the state school learning sector told my mum I'd never achieve anything, let alone pass any exams. My mum was determined and aimed to prove them wrong. I'm proud that I have a mum who had faith in me when others would not listen or gave up on me.

•   I can do anything if I put my mind to it: This is my own Autobiography; this is the book I had the independence to start and work on, the book that has let me pour out my internal pain and conflict, and finally has the power to help others. Without my mum's sacrifice and teaching me all the lessons, I never would have learned that, if I focus and believe in myself, I can achieve anything.

- Home-school is a threat: If enough parents saw the amazing benefits home-school gives to their child, there would be more home-school buildings being created, more kids being taken out of school, and more kids becoming successful than there are these days. Unfortunately for schools, this would mean that they would lose money, and therefore not a lot of schools will tell parents the true facts of home-school.

Some schools will even say home-schooling in the United Kingdom is illegal, when it is not. Home-school is one of the biggest threats to state schools, because if too many people decided to home-school, we would not need state schools any more, and more teachers would lose their jobs.

- Home-school helped my disabilities and their effects to be minimized for me. Some people wonder why kids come out of state school either the same or worse than they went in. This can be because teachers won't put the effort in to help your child improve, but still want them in there so they can be sure they will get paid. This is one of the biggest problems of the state school education system, and too many teachers get away with doing this. Some people/teachers may enjoy belittling or crushing your child's spirit too.

Therefore, it's very important that, if you don't want to home-school; you should at least be wary of which state school you put your child into and record exactly what they are doing with your child. Thanks to home-school, I feel it's helped my understanding of my disabilities, to know how to deal with them, and not to feel like I'm a freak of nature in the world. My mum showed me that I'm just as gifted, and should be just as respected and loved as everyone else, and for that I'm very thankful.

Analysis Thought: Chapter 9 Questionnaire for Parents: Parents Sacrifice

In this final analysis, I have decided to create a special questionnaire for parents who are thinking of home- schooling. By now you may be excited; others may be scared, some may even think that it's not for them. Sensing that this may come to your mind before finishing this book, I decided to provide this special questionnaire to help parents fully determine whether home- school may be for you or not. Maybe after this questionnaire, you may feel you want to do something different, the sacrifices you need to make may be too great, or you may still be propelled you to do it anyway. It's always best to go through the pros and cons before making a final decision.

This questionnaire, called 'Parents' Sacrifice', explains the things my mum had to sacrifice for me and my sister so we could have the very best in education and life. These are the main sacrifices, and everyone's sacrifice will be different. If you focus on the main ones, know the pros and know the cons, you can be assured that your final decision is the best one. My purpose in life is to help people, and by giving this questionnaire, I'm feeling happy that another of my main purposes is to help parents, and especially you who are reading this book, to the very end. Please take your time on the questionnaire, and it's important if you want to change an answer to change it, since it's all about you and what you feel you can do.

Questionnaire: Are you ready to home-school?

What are you prepared to sacrifice?

Personal Life
If you decide to home-school, your child's education is top priority. You may not be able to go out as much or relax during the day. As a home-school parent, the personal life you have now may change. You may have to focus on lessons, activities for the kids, help them with homework, and attend to their stresses and needs.

Pros
The child knows you're there, they will gain confidence, in future they may see what you have done for them and put in the effort to make good all that time and sacrifice for you. You will feel happier seeing your child succeeding more than they would have in state school and reap the rewards from it.

Cons
As a parent who has their own personal life, this can change drastically. You may not be able to do what you personally want to do. You may have to postpone going out with friends or even postponing your personal goals. You may go through more challenges and stress than the average adult. The fact that you may be around your child too much may stress you out as well.

Are you prepared to sacrifice this? Yes/No?

Love Life
If you're a single parent home-schooling, as my mum was, you will either have to be very careful who you introduce to your child, or accept that you may not be able to date for a long while. If you're not a single parent, you may face opposition from your spouse, who may not be ready to take on a big sacrifice with you. This can cause disagreements and even separation in the worst cases.

Pros
All focus is on the child. The home-school child won't have the worry of a new partner being in their lives or taking their parent away from them. There will be fewer issues relating to seeing broken relationships. If you spouse is alright with it, you will have the help of your spouse beside

you to help teach, or provide the finance for you, the children and home. You should also receive emotional support from them too in time of need and stress.

Cons
You may want to find a new partner, but may not have the time, energy or focus to concentrate on two people. You may want to speed-date, be taken on dates, or taken out by your partner. However, if you are home-schooling your child, (except for weekends) all focus must be on them and their lessons only. If you have a spouse, but they don't accept this, they might try to pressurise you to change your mind. Sometimes, in this case, you may have to prepare for separation, and if so, be prepared to home-school the child as a single mum or dad.

Are you prepared to sacrifice this? Yes/No?

Ridicule from family and friends.

You may see the gifts you child has, but others may not.

Pros
You will be doing the best you can and knowing you making the right choice for your child. All those people who ridiculed you and your child's success will see your child better, stronger and

more advanced than their kids. The best revenge in life is success. They may even come around and ask for your help and support on how to help and home-school their kids. You will be a splendid example for other people to follow.

Cons

People may pressurise you to forget home-schooling ideas, or tell you how they will affect the child negatively. They might belittle you, or even decide to separate from you, as well as not offer any support. You're going to have to have a body and heart of steel to face these people and deal with whatever they give you, for being different from the masses.

Are you prepared to sacrifice this? Yes/No?

Work and Employment

You either have the support of your spouse working with you, or you may have to depend on your own benefits/independent business to bring in all the money for what your child needs.

Pros
For my mum, she could find ways to get income flowing in, even though she could not take a job.

After she home-schooled me for nine years, she focused on developing her own business and, as a benefit, I'm able to help by being her personal advertiser, marketer, and giving her money to help whenever I can.

This can be one of the benefits you may receive in the future after your child is able to look after themselves.

Cons
You may not be able to go and work for a long time. If you decide to balance work and home-school, you may have to bring a babysitter in to care for your child.

Since all focus must be on the child and their education, it may be almost impossible to balance that with a regular job. You may have to depend on benefits, or what your spouse can give (whether you are divorced or together) to stay on track.

The best decision you get from the questionnaire is from your gut.

It doesn't matter if you got more no's then yes's; if you still feel like home-schooling, follow that gut. Everything happens for a reason, and doing the things you are most afraid of can give you more strength. The results you might fear may not be as severe as your mind is making them.

Final Tip to help make the Final Decision

Review your questionnaire, then ask yourself what will happen to your child if you decide to keep them in the state school or the condition they are in now? You must also review what will happen if you home-school them, because for the child, that might not be the right choice either. Write the answers down on paper and review them with your questionnaire. By this time, your final decision should arise.

Thank you so much for taking the time and energy to read this book. I'm sure you love your children, and want the best for your children. If you're a home-school child, I'm sure you want the best for yourself as well as guidance. It's important to remember that, no matter what, you can succeed from any type of system, and what people say about you does not make it a reality. I wish you luck on your journey through life and the journey of state education/home-school.

Good Luck!

Chapter 10: The Purpose of this Book

Writing is one of the most powerful means of communication which has ever been created on this earth. Although the traditional communication of letter writing has been rather lost due to the advancement of technology, it is still a precious gift, which has been taught to us by our elders and therefore should never be forgotten. I know the power of writing will never be forgotten by me. For writing, whether on paper or on the computer, has given me a confidence I never thought I had before, as well as a powerful tool to express myself during those times when I could not otherwise communicate.

From the age of six years old, I have always had a passion to write, whether it was non-fiction stories about my day to fictional stories about my toys and their magical adventures. I have an absolute passion to write, because for me it is an enjoyable experience. Once the first letter marks the paper or the first word enters on the document, ideas spring from my mind onto the paper like a jar full of marbles breaking and its marble contents spilling across the floor.

There are so many reasons to write this book. I want to bring the most important ones to light. Home-schooled, home-educated, educated otherwise, etc, are a few of the ways to express that your work is from another source, which is not in a school setting. However, what does 'home-schooled' mean? What is it all about? Is the environment of home-schooling the same as in an average state school? Well, this goes into one of my main reasons for writing this book, and that is to answer these puzzling questions for you, and to help you understand the concept of home-school in a clearer light. I notice that the subject of home-school is either misunderstood or seen in a different light, therefore, here are some of the reasons why I wanted to write this book.

• Home-school is rarely seen or spoken about I've noticed through research and going to libraries that there are many books on home-schooling, but they are rarely seen on the shelves, as well as home-school being rarely spoken about. It seems that these books on home-schooling are only found on the internet, and rarely ever found inside a library or book shop. Therefore, this makes the subject almost non-existent for people. Another interesting fact found while searching home-school books was...

- **The subject of home-school is more on "How to"**

Home-educate rather than the experience. It's good to have the knowledge of how to home-educate your child, but, what about the people who want to know what it is like for a child who is home-schooled? What's it like for him/her to live in it each day of their life until college, or until they decide that they are ready to leave that sort of education? How does it feel? Is it a blessing or a curse? Therefore, I decided to tell you this by sharing my story and experience of home-schooling with you in a set of chapters.

- **How?**

It's all good knowing the reason why I wanted to write a book on such a special subject as home-school, but how did it exactly come to be? What was needed? The most important thing I knew I needed to do when writing any kind of non-fiction book, or assignment, was to...

- **Research**

Research is the key to writing any type of book. There was no way I could have just written my life story down, without any sort of background information on the actual subject of home-schooling.

Many types of home-schooling have the same name but have different meanings. For example, Autonomous Learning and

Auto-didacticism mean that the student takes care of their own responsibilities and career paths, but Autonomous Learning is a home-school organization; that sees their students as individual people who are responsible for their own learning and career paths, while Auto-didacticism just means "to learn on your own" or "a self-taught person".

Although those two are somewhat similar, Auto-didacticism is not an education organization. Another important fact I realised I needed was...

- **The passion to write**

Great authors wrote with a passion, writing their stories in detail, bringing out the characters and the atmosphere vividly. After reading their books, I felt a sense of nostalgia in me, because it felt like all those great characters, which were my friends, were leaving, and I wanted the story to continue so much.

Although my story is not fiction at all, I still want to bring my story vividly to life and share every single detail and memories with you about my home-school experience from childhood to teenage years. I want you to experience what

I did and fully understand the perspective of a home-schooled child, who went through all a primary school's harsh times, to the tasks and strains of home-school life, and that is the passion that has made me write this book.

- **Purpose**

If you're new to home-school, or already a home-schooled person, hopefully through reading this book, and by the end of this book, you will...

- Prepare yourself for home-school ups and downs.

- Protect yourself against the oddities of home- schooling, and learn how to deal with society's prejudices towards it.

- Know how to explain the meaning of home-school to others, who don't truly understand it.

- Be proud of your home-school education and not feel like an outcast because of it.

As for the people who are not home-educated or who have little knowledge of the experience, I hope through reading this book and by the end you will...

- Have a better understanding of home-school

- Not take a negative view about home-schoolers and their lives.

- Understand the reasons why some children need to be taken out of school.

- Uncover home-school myths and find the actual truths to counter them.

Thank You

I would just like to thank you, the reader, for buying this book and taking the time to read my story. Without the readers, I am not sure where this book would be.

I would also like to thank my dear mother, whom I love very much, and I am so thankful and grateful for having. Thank you mum for taking me out of a school, where I couldn't grow; plus, thank you for going through battles and stress, just so I can stand on my two feet without shame. Without you mum I would not be the person I am now. Also, I would like to thank my sister for supporting me in times of need and, finally, thank the whole family on my mother's side, for accepting me for who I am and not neglecting me.

Thank you.

THE END

References/Web Links

Chapter 1
(minddisorders.com, 2012, Mixed ReceptiveExpressive Language Disorder, http://www.minddisorders.com/Kau-Nu/Mixed-receptive-expressive-language-disorder.html Sunday 25th March 2012)

(http://autism.lovetoknow.com, 2006-2013, What is Atypical Autism? http://autism.lovetoknow.com/What Is Atypical Autism, Wednesday 20th March 2013)

(http://www.specialeducationalneeds.co.uk, 2005-2013, Atypical Autism, http://www.specialeducationalneeds.co.uk/UsefulInformation/TypesofSEN-Disability/Atypical%20Autism.html, Wednesday 20th March 2013)

Chapter 3
(wikihow.com, 2012, How to respond to an adult bully, http://www.wikihow.com/Respond-to-an-Adult-Bully, Wednesday 20th June 2012) 193

Chapter 4
Conumdrumland, 2009, http://www.whatsyourconundrum.com/general/is-this-childabuse-would-you-call-cps, Wednesday 11th July 2012)

(Photo-dictonary.com, 2012, breaking rope, http:// www.photo-dictionary.com/ phrase/9191/breakingrope.html, Wednesday 11th July 2012)

Chapter 5
(Uaddit.com, 2000-2012, Autodidactic Learning, http://uaddit.com/discussions/showthread.php?t=7214, Thursday 19th July 2012)

(Wikipedia.org, 2012, Autodidaticsim, http://en.wikipedia.org/wiki/Autodidacticism, Thursday 19th July 2012)

(Wikipedia.org, 2012, Home-schooling, http://en.wikipedia.org/wiki/Home-schooling, Thursday 19th July 2012)
(Knoji.com, 2012,

Types of Home-schooling, http:// home-schooling.knoji.com/types-of-homeschooling/, Thursday 19th July 2012)
(LBL, 2009,

Different types of Home-schooling, http://www.lblesd.k12.or.us/home-school/different_types.php, Thursday 19th July 2012)
(thestar.com,1995-2012,

Different Types 194 of Home-schooling, http://thestar.com. my/news/story. asp?fi le=/2004/8/1/ education/8544063 HYPERLINK "http://thestar. com.my/ news/story.asp?fi le=/2004/8/1/ education/8544063&sec=education"& HYPERLINK "http://thestar.com.my/ news/story.asp?fi le=/2004/8/1/ /8544063&sec=education"sec=education, Thursday 19th July 2012) (mamashealth.com, 2000-2012,

Different Types of Home-schooling, http:// www.mamashealth.com/ home-school/, Thursday 19th July 2012)

(http://patfarenga.squarespace.com, 2010, Celebrity Unschoolers, http://patfarenga. squarespace. com/pat-farengas- blog/2010/8/10/celebrityunschoolers.html, Saturday 9th March 2013)

(http://home-schooling.knoji.com/, 2013, Types of Home-schooling, http://home-schooling. knoji.com/ types-of-home-schooling/, Saturday 9th March 2013) (http://www.oxfordhome-schooling.co.uk, 2010, Home-schooling and the Law, http://www.oxfordhome-schooling.co.uk/general/homeschooling-the-law/, Saturday 9th March 2013) 195

(Answers.com, 2013 What Year did Home-schooling Start?, wiki.answers.com/Q/What year did homeschooling start, Saturday 9th March 2013)

(http://www.education.com, 2006-2013, Homeschooling, http://www.education.com/reference/ article/home-schooling1/, Saturday 9th March 2013)

Chapter 6
(http://www.home-ed-magazine.com, 2013, Home Education, http://www.home-ed-magazine.com/ INF/STRT/strt_faq.html, Sunday 24th March 2013

(http://www.superscholar.org/, 2011, Can Homeschooling be a Handicap?, http://www.superscholar. org/can-home-schooling-be-a-handicap/, Sunday 24th March 2013)

(http://home-schooling.gomilpitas.com, 2003-013, dispelling the Stereotype of Ethnic Prejudice in Homeschooling, http://home-schooling.gomilpitas.com/ articles/071003.htm#.UU6vszfNJeF, Sunday 24th March 2013)

(http://home-schooling.gomilpitas.com, 19972013, Afro centric Home-schooling, http://homeschooling.gomilpitas.com/religion/afrocentric.htm#.UU65YjfNJeE, Sunday 24th March 2013)

Appendix

This section is where I recommend the best books and websites for you or your home-school child.

Home-school and Autism/PDD/Aspersers Syndrome

• Home-schooling the Child with Aspergers Syndrome: Real Help for Parents Anywhere and On Any Budget, by Lise Pyles. Published by: Jessica Kingsley, 2004. ISBN: 1843107619

• Home-schooling the Child with Autism: Answers to the Top Questions Parents and Professionals Ask, by Jeanette McAfee, Patricia Schetter and Kandis Lighthall. Published by: Jossey Bass, 2009. ISBN: 0470295263

Home-school and Learning
• Khan Academy
• www.Coursera.org

Recommended Books
• The Complete Reader, by Neville Goddard. Published by: Audio Enlightenment, 2013. ISBN: 099109140X

- The Secret Series: 4 Books Collection Set Pack: Hero, The Secret, The Power and The Magic, by Rhonda Byne, 2013. ISBN: 3200329106

- Think and Grow Rich, by Napoleon Hill. Published by: Wilder Publications, 2007. ISBN: 1934451355

- The Alchemist: A Fable About Following Your Dream, by Paulo Coelho. Published by: HarperTorch, 2006. ISBN: 0061233846

Follow Your Dreams

Follow Your Dreams is a national charity with our head office based in South Wales, established in 2004 to support children and young people with learning disabilities.

We believe that every young person has the right to maximise their potential. Far too often, albeit with the best intentions, children with learning disabilities are instilled with the belief that they are limited in what they can achieve. This leaves them demotivated, afraid to try new things, trapped in their comfort zone. We work with them and their families fostering a 'can do' attitude and developing their skills. We encourage them to recognise their skills and potential, empowering and motivating a change in attitude, providing hope aspirations and opportunities.

We support volunteer led community groups to set up from conception, through to constitution, legal and financial support. Our groups meet up weekly, and we currently have 9 groups operational throughout South Wales and South West England, reaching some 388 families. All our clubs are run by volunteers with the support of the Charity. The aim is that each group will be self-financing within two years.

Groups retain their independence in operational matters but have the reassurance, administration, financial and governance support of our Charity.

Bi-annually we provide tickets to families through our partnership with Circus Starr, the circus was created for children who are new to the spectacle of live performance or struggle to sit and concentrate, animal free with no scary clowns!

Thanks to our friends at Bluestone Resorts Wales, we are able to provide last minute accommodation free of charge to families with learning disabilities. For many this will be the only break these families get! We also arrange an outward-bound activity weekend at Macaroni Woods for families with learning disabilities and their siblings.

In 2016, we opened our very first Charity Shop and Tea Room to provide a much-needed income stream, fundraising is getting tough, grant funding non-existent. But most importantly, has provided volunteering and training opportunities for young people with learning disabilities to gain valuable work experience in our shops. Named after our community Young Ambassador Rosie, our dream is to open further shops across the UK.

In 2017, we formed Birthday Smiles which is supported by volunteer parents. We receive nominations of children to receive cards. We post the child's photograph, their age that month, and a brief description of them in a Facebook group. Supporters of the group then send birthday cards for the following month to our head office address and we batch send them to the child in time for their birthday. No personal information is passed out online for example the full date of birth or home address, school details etc.

LifeWise formed in 2018 is our weekly project run in South Wales, which brings together youngsters with learning disabilities 18+ who are not in employment or education to partake in activities including Arts & Crafts, Health and Well-being, Heritage, Knowledge/Life Skills and Performing Arts. The purpose of the project is to help these young people overcome these barriers, focusing on health and wellbeing throughout.

We have just 6 staff based at our headquarters covering the whole of our UK operations. Therefore, we rely on the work of our incredible volunteers who are the heart of our charity. Our volunteers are at the heart of all our work, they make an enormous difference and are committed to the passion to help children and young people with learning disabilities. They supplement the work our employees do and also take the lead on service delivery in our community groups, as well as fund-raise for us in a variety of ways.

To get involved, call us on 01443 218443 or email info@followyourdreams.org.uk

Follow Your Dreams Charity
www.followyourdreams.org.uk

Facebook: FollowYourDreamsCharity
Twitter: @tweetfyd

www.ingramcontent.com/pod-product-compliance
Lightning Source LLC
Chambersburg PA
CBHW071438080526
44587CB00014B/1901